P9-CRN-017

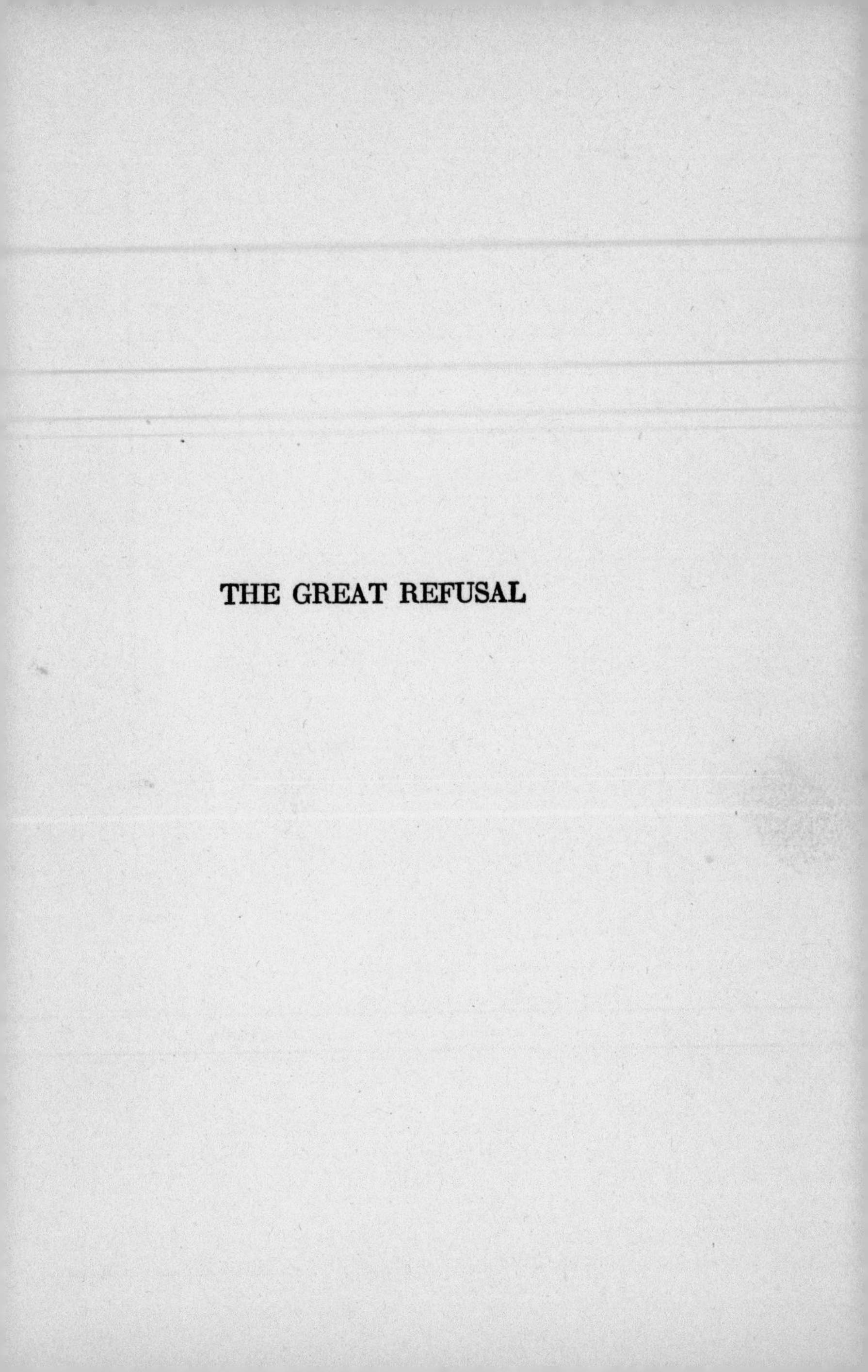

THE GREAT REFUSAL

By

NEWELL DWIGHT HILLIS

The Great Refusal
And Other Evangelistic Sermons.

A Man's Value to Society
Studies in Self-Culture and Character.

The Investment of Influence
Studies in Social Sympathy and Service.

Great Books as Life-Teachers
Studies of Character, Real and Ideal.

The Contagion of Character
Studies in Culture and Success.

Great Men as Prophets of a New Era
Studies in Personality and Power.

The Battle of Principle
Heroism and Eloquence of Anti-Slavery Conflict.

German Atrocities

The Blot on the Kaiser's 'Scutcheon

Rebuilding Europe in the Face of World-Wide Bolshevism

All the Year Round
Sermons for Church and Civic Celebrations.

BOOKLETS

Foretokens of Immortality

How the Inner Light Failed

Right Living as a Fine Art

The Master of the Science of Right Living

The School in the Home

EDITED BY DOCTOR HILLIS

Lectures and Orations by Henry Ward Beecher

The Great Refusal

AND OTHER EVANGELISTIC SERMONS

By

NEWELL DWIGHT HILLIS

NEW YORK CHICAGO

Fleming H. Revell Company

LONDON AND EDINBURGH

New York: 158 Fifth Avenue
Chicago: 17 North Wabash Ave.
London: 21 Paternoster Square
Edinburgh: 75 Princes Street

Foreword

AMONG the difficulties of present-day preaching is the fact that the press, the platform, the college, even business and finance, have become competitors of the pulpit. Centuries ago the people of ancient Israel overheard Saul, the son of Kish, warning a group of servants that it was folly to make war upon God. In their astonishment, the people exclaimed, "Is Saul also among the prophets?" It is a distinct gain for society that laymen are warning our people against lawlessness, luxury, and frivolity, since any movement that calls the people back to the faith of the founders and fathers, makes for social betterment. One thing, however, is still left to the preacher,—moral passion, passion for men, and it is this passion that turns the pulpit into a throne. In the belief that the issues of life and death for modern society are in the pulpit, John Ruskin once called the sermon, "thirty minutes to raise the dead in."

These sermons are sparks struck out on the anvil of events. They are here given as they were spoken. In his book, *The Black Arrow,* Stevenson tells us that a soldier in the thick of the fight, fitted his arrow to the bow, and let the shaft fly against the enemy, without stopping to ask whether the point was polished, or the feathers beautiful. These chapters, plain, simple and unadorned, represent addresses that were given in the hope of winning an immediate decision, and inducing some noble youth to burn his bridges behind him, and to swear instant fidelity to the convictions of the Christian religion, for God's sake and for man's.

N. D. H.

Plymouth Church,
Brooklyn, N. Y.

Contents

I

THE GREAT REFUSAL

"When the young man heard that saying, he went away sorrowful."—MATT. xix: 22.

THE rich young ruler is one of the most fascinating figures in the New Testament. In disposition he was most lovable, in manners most attractive, in manhood most praiseworthy. He had the serious temper, also, that is the first sign of greatness in youth. He was reverent in spirit, he had a hungry mind, he was eager, ingenuous and courteous, being altogether admirable. From the moment Jesus saw him, the Master loved this rich, young ruler. Indeed, the words that describe His affection for the youth are the words used to describe His love for John, the Beloved Disciple. There are two kinds of friendship; there is an exterior friendship based on neighbourhood, commercial partnership or political plans; there is an interior friendship, in which two men sympathise along the same lines, enjoy the same intellectual tastes, hate the same wrongs, cherish the same political and moral ideals; then friends coalesce like drops of water, becoming one. Jesus first tested this youth, to make sure of his worth, and then, widening His little inner circle, made a place for this young ruler.

Every generation has one outstanding figure. When this young Carpenter, who held the heart of the people in His hand, made an overture of friendship to the rich young ruler, what an opportunity was that which passed before the ambitious youth! Addressing his judges, Socrates exclaimed: "At what price would one not estimate an hour's converse with Homer or Hesiod!" But at what price would a youth, who aspired to be a leader of his time, not estimate the opportunity of daily converse with the greatest religious leader of any age or clime! Jesus was the one man of moral genius of His epoch! What an overture was His to this youth to become one of the charter members and founders of Christ's "Beloved Society," His "League of Pity," an institution destined to outlive all the cities and empires of that era! One would have rejoiced to have seen the young ruler rise up, fling away his baubles, forsake all and follow this Master to influence, fame and blessing. But something blinded his eyes, and cast a glamour over his vision. The jewel slipped between his fingers. He tossed the gold away. It is as Dante has said: "Who is that nameless one, gnawed with remorse?" While Virgil answers: "Let us flee! That is the youth who made the Great Refusal."

Consider the reasonableness of Christ's command. It was not a question of the rich, young ruler's salvation, but of his perfection and world-wide influence. Ambitious for spiritual supremacy, the youth asked, "What shall I do to be perfect?" For this was one of those noble and occasional spirits not content with the better, but longing for the best. It is one thing to be saved, so as by fire. It is quite another thing to come home like a prince from victorious wars, when all the hosts come out to meet and greet the leader. No question about his integrity; he had kept all the commandments from his youth up. The problem was a problem of influence, how to make his gold, offices and honours to journey out into all the world. Jesus was showing him how to make his name immortal, how to make his influence shine like a star, that would never die out of the world's sky. He bade him do the rare, wonderful and godlike thing. The youth seems to have been one of those gifted souls who can sacrifice and lift themselves up, one able to dwell apart from and above his fellows. But when he had gazed upon the vision of ideal perfection and immortal influence, the young man stood long in silence, and then, wistfully, shook his head, and sorrowfully went away.

It is said that "he was sorrowful"—not startled, not angry, not embittered. His reason approved Christ's counsel—otherwise he would have contradicted Jesus. His judgment affirmed the practicability of Jesus, otherwise he would have gone away mocking the dreamer. But Jesus was right. His own heart condemned him. At last, silently and sadly, the youth turned away.

Having made overtures to rude fishermen, publicans and peasants, Jesus now makes an overture to a youth of wealth, address, of office and social position. He plans to bring an entirely new element into the apostolic band. "If thou wilt be perfect (not if thou wilt be saved), go and sell all that thou hast, and distribute to the poor—then come and follow me." To understand the genius of the overture we must translate the command into terms of modern life. Let us seek out in thought the son of some modern multi-millionaire, representing railways or oil or steel. Let his annual income amount to millions, as a few there are today. Let the youth, restless in his silken palace, cast about for a higher life. In obedience to the heavenly vision, suppose this rich young American should appear some morning in the directors' room of a great corporation and say: "I wish my one hundred million dollar fortune to be set aside in the interest of the ten thousand workmen in our shops. Let all the dividends for myself be distributed to the workingmen as weekly wages." Then suppose the youth should sell his father's palace and live himself in one of the company's houses, all bare, gaunt and squalid. Suppose also that in the spirit, not of paternalism, but of fraternalism, not of lordly benevolence, but of true brotherliness, that this youth should become the burden bearer for these poor people, being medicine for their sickness, staff for their weakness, a comforter in their sorrows. And when, having broken his very life for them, the youth falls on death, it will be for these thousands of workingmen as if the sun itself were eclipsed, and joy had been struck dead.

Now there can be only one result—these working people will take their children to his grave, to whisper his name, to tell the story of his beauty, to pledge their boys to emulate his life. Would not our world then have another name to charm by? Would not the name of this youth become a guiding star for the pilgrim host? And his influence be like a bow bent to send his teachings straight into the hearts of men? One such deed in American society would recivilise this nation, and transform the ideals of our generation. There are a hundred heirs to vast American fortunes today, but where is there one of whom Dante will not have to say, "When some among them I had recognised, I beheld among them him who, through cowardice, made the Great Refusal?" Now, this was exactly what Christ asked the rich young ruler to do. Had that rich young ruler followed Jesus, who, being rich, for our sakes made Himself poor, orators would have winged their arrows with his name, poets would have adorned their pages with his example, statesmen would have used his career as an inspiration for reform, millions of men would have gone to him for help and guidance, as pilgrims turn toward a fountain bubbling in a desert, or a date palm waving in the wilderness. He threw away his opportunity, therefore Dante placed him among "the exiles of eternity."

For Jesus, living was a very serious business. The pursuit of perfection was life's supreme end, and surrender to the right the one secret of happiness. "Go sell all, give to the poor. Come, follow me, and together we will go about and do good." Choose between life on the one hand, and martyrdom like Paul's on the other. The choice is clear, definite and final. Paul had to decide, and he forsook his father's house, his office in the Sanhedrim, his wealth and friends, and followed Christ, to mobs in Ephesus, stones in Lystra and the headsman's axe in Rome. For reward Christ gave Paul a thousandfold more through happiness in the life that now is, and influence through the next nineteen centuries. Polycarp had his choice between dying in his bed, and the martyr's funeral pile; he chose the chariot of flame, and that is why his name still is a beacon fire across the sea of time. Galileo had to make his choice—the rack on the one side, science and the moving sun on the other, and Galileo chose.

What? Hate one's own family! This is unnatural, cruel and against the higher reason. But yesterday when that mother returned to find the house in flames and realised that her babe was sleeping in the cradle, she flung aside the neighbours who restrained her, pushed back the older children who clutched at her garments, hated the officer who was a barrier between herself and her babe, and forsook all to follow her child, and snatch it from the jaws of death, and bring it to safety. It was this hating her stronger children for the moment that saved the weaker babe, and makes the mother's name and deed divine. What? Hate your own household? When this splendid youth, living in his father's mansion, the favourite of society, who has a golden key for the door to all great houses and is sought for everywhere, finds a true daughter of the people, and loves her, and wakens from his dream to discover that his wealthy parents say "No, she is of a lower station," and his friends whisper, "It will never do," and advise caution and prudence—does not the man, if there is a spark of manhood in him, rise up, shake off all restraints, become the builder of his own fortune, and the author of a happiness beyond all dreams, simply because he obeys the highest law, the law of love? This is praiseworthy in daily life. It is also admirable and divine when Christ commands men so to do.

But just what the rich ruler declined to do, Jesus did. With divine forethought Jesus laid out the plan of His life, and adhered inflexibly to that plan. Influence must be achieved. Fame is bought at great price. The man who would have a name that the world would not willingly let die, must pay for what he wants. The law of compensation forbids deceit in this matter of influence. Jesus stood up against the storm of temptation and sin, took all the blows, suffered the bruises, was marred in His face, pierced in His body, crushed and broken inside and out, but He never flinched from His duty. He did right, always right; He sacrificed, always sacrificed; He served others, never Himself; He died subduing His pain and praying for His enemies, and so bought the Name that is above every name. No candidate for influence can achieve supremacy over men's minds and hearts, in any other way than Christ's way. Experts can juggle coin out of other men's pockets into their own, but there are no tricks by which men can have ease and, by juggling, secure influence. No virtue unasked comes knocking at man's door trying to force an entrance. No heroism comes unurged, for men do not fall heir to influence. Perfection costs, even in the lower realms. The great singer is born with a high dome in his throat, and with flexible vocal chords, but for ten years he must work like a slave, and, as an artist, toil on to keep the voice he has built. Is the youth ambitious for fame as an artist? Then hard work is her only hope.

Remember Millet and Turner, their poverty, their drudgery, the thousands of canvases they destroyed, the rising at daylight, the night falling to find them still at their task; the broken health, the unappreciative public, then sudden darkness and death, and still no recognition! Ah! but they had the consciousness of perfection, and knew they had founded a great school and that the time would come when nations would compete for a canvas. For each Millais and Turner it pays to sell all their goods and follow the arts, for the sake of perfect beauty and truth. There is nothing great in man but his soul. The candidate for immortal fame, —Milton, Scott, or Stevenson,—must be willing to slave for perfection in his art; and think you that character is not something worth struggling for unto blood and death? Why, a great poem or statue, a great drama or cathedral are rags over against the gold and ivory of truth and justice, purity and love. The one candidate ends his career, saying, "Here is my book"; another, "Here is my song"; another, "Here is my loom and ship"; another, "Here is my law." At last one comes saying, "Here are thy little ones, redeemed. I have been so busy saving them that I have had no chance to save my own soul, and I am not worthy to come in." And lo, this one hath an abundant entrance, for at great price hath he bought his influence and his salvation.

When Jesus commanded this youth to seek righteousness and character first, and gold and office and pleasure afterward, He emphasized a principle that our generation needs to ponder and obey. Our people are all but insane in their wild pursuit of show, equipage, and sensuous delights. The orgies of our New Year's Eve celebration are beginning to be commented upon even in foreign countries. An English traveller, describing what he saw in the New York hotels, says that Americans have outdone Lucullus, the Sybarite, with his feasts, and that the only thing he missed in New York restaurants was the emetic and the second dinner. A New York *chef,* whose salary makes the pay of our Supreme Court judges, our governors and our educators seem paltry, is now in despair because he fears our feasts have reached their limit. He can conceive of no more decorations, he can discover no new meats, he knows no new drinks, for the goal has been reached. But in Paris they have tried a new way to intensify the taste of rich foods.

These epicureans, whose supreme pursuit is fleshly pleasure, have connected the diners and the foods with electric wires, and a gentle voltage passing through the food and the tongue has intensified the taste, making the wines richer, the ices sweeter, the nectarine more delicious. But the result was what might have been expected. The next day all foods for the Sybarite were tasteless as sawdust. Long time passed before the tongue recovered its normal power. To such an extreme has our generation come through the pursuit of rich foods, beautiful dress, brilliant equipage, show and splendour. Nothing is more trite than for me to say that any man who spent $20 on his New Year's dinner would have had far higher pleasure to have sought out some poor seamstress, working for a sweater, and purchased for the widow and her little children, flour and bread and meat that would have fed the orphans for a month, and brought a burst of sunshine into a dark tenement. Sensualism never pays. Epicureanism is a lie. Show and glitter burn the soul like sulphuric acid sprinkled on roses and lilies. Character is first, then pleasure, office and honour. If the fathers have tried the life of the Sybarite and broken their hearts why should the children take the same cup of flame into their hands and break *their* hearts? Strange that two generations insist on stubbing their toes on the same obstruction in life's path! The body is not a sensual harp, with physical nerves that are strings to be played upon by Bacchus and Venus. It is a mere under-servant, whose strength is to be translated into terms of service by those goddesses named the Angel of Sacrifice, the Angel of Suffering, the Angel of Humility and the Angel of Love.

At first blush, the rich young ruler seems to have acted upon considerations of prudence and sound judgment. For the moment it seemed as if Jesus were asking him to wreck his whole earthly career. The gist of the matter is in this—he must have had notable gifts of mind and disposition, but, being young, he had become a ruler because he was rich. Tradition and precedent had decreed that only old men could be rulers, in Israel. But this rich young ruler had turned longing eyes toward the Sanhedrim. So skilfully had he handled his gold, his social position and political influence, that all precedents were overthrown, and he was made a ruler. And yet spiritual supremacy asked for the mellow judgment, the ripe reason, and the gentle spirit. Some things cannot be forced—the ripening of wheat, the mellowing of apples, the maturing of souls. A young judge can condemn a criminal, and with iron justice hang the wretch; it is given to an old man to transform a bad man into a good man. It is better to heal the soul than to break the body. Young men for leadership in war, young men for railways and factories, and fleets of ships; but we want no immaturity on the bench, where justice and spiritual supremacy rule. What nothing else can do for the intellect and the heart, time, experience, and age can accomplish. Outwardly the rich young man had achieved his ambition and was enthroned with the gray-haired members of the highest court in Jerusalem. And Jesus told the rich young ruler plainly that he did not ring true. To be a ruler, was more than seeming to be one. There was the note of unreality in a young man, however able, with his inexperience, wishing to do an old man's work. He had the experience of twenty summers, but needed the experience of seventy ripe and rounded years.

It is one thing for a man to be a soldier of the British Guards surviving a hundred battles and winning the coveted Victoria Cross when his comrades carried the hero off the field of battle. It is quite another thing for a rich youth to go to an Old Soldiers' Home and with gold buy an aged hero's Victoria Cross, and pin it on his coat. The rich young ruler was decorated with a medal that he had never won upon the battlefield of the soul. When the young ruler asked Jesus what he should do to be perfect, the answer was quick and searching: "Strike the note of reality. But for your gold, you would never have been elected a ruler. You have not earned the right to sit in judgment on other men's souls. If you would be perfect, give your gold to the poor, and achieve the maturity, the mellowness, that love for the poor alone can give. Come with Me. Together we will search out the heartbroken, feed the hungry, save the prodigal, be light to the darkened, be life to the dead. There must be no schism in the soul. You must not be young and inexperienced, and seem to arrogate to yourself maturity, and the right to judge older and wiser men."

How reasonable the counsel! How just! and how generous, too! The rich young ruler was outwardly sound, but inwardly he had played the prodigal. Oh, how we long to see him rise up, and, forsaking all, join the lowly Galilæan! What an opportunity he lost! He might have been the great apostle to launch Christ's enterprise. This youth had perhaps the position and the genius that fitted him to have divided honours with Paul. He might have saved the early Church from a century of persecution, and its baptism of blood and fire. When Don Francisco de Xaviero heard the call, he left his gold and his castle, and became immortal forever, as the sainted Xavier. But this youth—ah, the gold slips between his fingers down into the sea! And little wonder that Dante fled from the youth who made the Great Refusal!

Searching out the reasons for the ruler's refusal, we find one in the vastness of the enterprise proposed. For a rich and successful young man, it seemed an impossible thing to give away his wealth and wreck his career. The youth's property came by inheritance. He was born to be a popular leader. His strongest gift was with men, and not over things. Jesus knew that he would never be happy until he used his supreme talent. A bird is perfectly contented with walking on two legs, until the morning when it finds out it has wings. From that hour, wings make legs contemptible. The youth was satisfied with money and business, until he wakened, felt the stirrings of higher gifts, and discovered that he must work for men and with men. But the closing of the door on worldly success behind him was too hard. He seemed to himself like a child, who was asked to carry the world on his shoulders, like Atlas. Imagination every hour increased the magnitude of the task Jesus had outlined. Last night the moon yonder in the sky seemed like a world of silver, swimming in a sea of amethyst. And larger still was that new world that suddenly rose on the horizon of this young man's imagination. But the argument was not valid, nor was the youth sincere. Jesus did not call him to immediate perfection. He called him to the next duty, and bade him take the next step.

Christ is not unreasonable. He asks only one step at a time. He gives strength for today's burden—no more. He gives light for today's path—no more. "Give us this day our daily bread"—not bread for five years from today. He sends help, never too soon—that is our safety; never too late—that is our salvation. The first step along the path Christ pointed out was no harder for the youth than the first step he took along the line of his own selfishness and ease. The Christian life is a reasonable life, a natural life, a beautiful life and an easy life, as well as a heroic and hard one. There is a great chasm that separates the babe from the statesman, the sage and the poet, but the child grows so naturally, by taking a step at a time, that suddenly this boy, Isaac Newton, wakes up to find himself a scientist, full of years and honours. It can never be reasonable to refuse to obey Christ because of the difficulties of the Christian life, or the vastness of the enterprise, until a child is justified in refusing to go to school because it is a great undertaking to be a scholar; to refuse to become a clerk because it is a weighty matter to be a merchant or manufacturer. Every consideration of reason rebukes the young ruler for refusing obedience because of the magnitude of the life proposed.

Unconsciously, also, the rich young ruler was influenced by the desire to postpone the decision. The one duty of the moment was instant action, while delay lost all. He had no power to cast himself fully into Christ's cause. He failed by not taking his courage into his hand. The difference between two young men of equal gifts is the difference of will, decision and instant resolution. We have all known young men of great promise, courteous manners, fine natural gifts, ripe culture, who just miss success. A friend goes to them with a splendid opening. And the man says: "That seems just the opening I want. I will look into it at once." When a month has passed by, and the opportunity has gone, then the youth wakes up, and decides to act. There are men who remember the treasures in the orchard immediately after the robins have picked the last red cherry. The world is full of moulders, who decide upon the pattern an hour after the iron has cooled. Yesterday, Opportunity knocked at the man's door, and day after tomorrow he will decide to arise and open to the stranger, to discover that she has gone forever. To the farmer comes a strange conjunction of events in May, and soil and sun and seed conspire, but he who postpones to July need not expect that October will postpone also her time for harvest. The men who fail in the world have not failed because God and Nature did not give them success. When the ruby-hot glass runs like water, that is the time to pour it into the mould. Not a second must be lost. The true man acts at the first note of duty. The successful man bestirs himself at the first overture of opportunity. Life is large, but it has no room for delay. What robbed this youth of fame and immortal influence? The answer is clear—delay, indecision, and drifting until a more convenient time.

Perhaps the youth was in the mood when it was easier to dream than to change moral impressions and ideas into actions. Nothing is easier to form than the habit of spiritual reverie. Some natures there are that exhale aspirations like clouds. But the desert lands of Sahara are not cloudless lands—the skies above the hot sands are often overcast, only the white clouds are too high, and never condense into raindrops. Years ago, in Paris, I made the round of the American studios. One day an artist-friend took me into a garret. Going up the steps he told me that he would show me the most glorious dreamer in France. I found the low ceiling covered with pencil sketches; every inch of the walls and the very floor plastered over with outlines. Every morning found the artist at his canvas. In one ceaseless procession the visions passed before him—angels, seraphs, sunsets, trees, castles, scarred cliffs, golden clouds, palace, hut, canoe, ocean steamer, mound, volcano, peasant, prince, tropic luxuries—a thousand sketches—not one of them complete. A thousand dreams and faces in the air, but no power to pin them down to a canvas, and fix them there forever. No artist had more glorious visions of beauty, but men with one-tenth the imaginative power painted ten times the number of pictures, and had a hundred times the income. The artist who indulged in his dreams lived on his reveries; he was like multitudes, who dream their dreams of ideal perfection, plan noble deeds of helpfulness, but do practically almost nothing. For years they have been going to join the church, but they have never aligned themselves with the forces of right. For other years they have had their hours when they planned what they would do for Christ's poor and weak, but these are still only clouded aspirations. And now, the visions are beginning to die away. No longer is the heart agitated with joyous tumult at the thought of Jesus Christ, and His overtures of friendship. No longer does the pulse beat high with hope at the sound of His footprints and the stroke of the Divine Stranger knocking at the door. For the harvest is passed and the summer is ended, and they are not saved. They have made the Great Refusal.

The early traditions tell us that this youth who went away sad, could not stay away, but returned. His refusal haunted him, the vision of immortal influence tormented his spirit, and at last he rose up and returned to the Master. Some scholars tell us that the rich young man was Lazarus, who lived at Bethany, and that he was among the first of the martyrs. But we question the tradition. Some have thought that the rich young ruler was Saul, who at length became bitter toward his Master, and finally, to justify himself, wrought out the persecution, and killed Stephen. But it seems incredible that Paul should not have recalled the saddest hour in his life, the hour when he made the Great Refusal. We conclude, therefore, that this rich young ruler never found his opportunity again. His name has perished. His influence has passed like the morning dew. His work and career were as evanescent as a driftinfi cloud. His name might have been one to charm by, but he perished like the falling leaf, leaving a warning, alas, how searching!

Oh, all ye young hearts, have ye not drifted long enough? For years you have postponed the great decision. Will you once more make the Great Refusal?

Are there none in whom the wells of feeling are choked up? Are there none who begin to chafe under the fetters of habit and passion, and long for deliverance? Are you not weary of your restlessness? Are you not ready to exchange storm and tumult for the calm of the harbour? If sins have uprooted your life as storms have broken some goodly tree, will you not remember that the Husbandman is abroad in His world garden, and that once more the south wind may blow softly through the broken branches? To you this day comes Opportunity. Today all the moments are big with fate. Oh! Listen to the voice:

"Master of human destinies am I.
Fame, love and fortune on my footsteps wait.
And passing by,
Hovel and mart and palace, soon or late,
I knock unbidden once at every gate.
If sleeping, wake; if feasting, rise before
I turn away. It is the hour of fate.
All those who doubt or hesitate
Seek me in vain, and uselessly implore.
I answer not, and I return no more."

II

WHAT IF ALL GOD'S GIFTS BE IN VAIN?

"I am afraid of you, lest I have bestowed upon you labour in vain."—GAL. iv: 11.

THIS is Paul's last plea—the plea of Love! Fearing lest some whom he had hoped to win were about to turn away forever, Paul called in all his reserves, and forced a decision. Pathetic indeed that tremulous appeal, burdened with love and tears. The scarred hero knew that his life work was now all but done. Certain last words must be spoken. Looking out upon the multitude of faces that he knew, he remembers that some men had been won while others had stood out, unyielding to the very last. In that moment every great thing in Paul's nature rose up into its full estate, and he became, as it were, a hundred men! He appealed unto self-interest: "Godliness is profitable in the life that now is." He appealed unto reason: "The noble prophets, heroes and martyrs are come to full flower and fruit in Jesus." He appeals to affection: "The love of Christ constraineth you." He strikes the note of fear and alarm: "Be not deceived; God is not mocked; for whatsoever a man soweth that shall he also reap."

Every bell in his belfry rings, but with strokes,

oh! how different! The ringers in a cathedral tower ring their chimes in divers ways. Now the quick notes peal out the wedding march! Then, with slow and stately stroke they boom out solemn accompaniment to inaugural address and majestic ceremonial! Sometimes, at the midnight hour, they strike quick, sharp blows; sparks that suggest flames, as they startle a sleeping city to terror and alarm. Not otherwise Paul sounds his bell to waken men.

But when Paul has stated the argument from history, the argument from experience, the argument from the uniqueness of Christ, and emphasized motives that are personal, suddenly he realises that if he has succeeded in winning some, others stand forth, hard and unyielding. And then comes this piercing, grief-stricken exclamation: "I have done all that man can do; but what if my all should be in vain?"

All faithful workers want to win success. No strong man who has put forth his full labour can easily confront approaching failure. We have seen some men preserve youth into their extreme age, because they toil amidst an atmosphere of victory. Others we have seen grow old before their time because of the inner consciousness of failure. But the servant is not above his master, and Paul, who was sent, is not above Him who sends the messenger. If five times Paul confesses the fear that his work has been in vain, yet His Master so felt before him. What pathos and tragedy in Christ's struggle to win His twelve disciples! For three years He laboured for them, after the pattern of earth's most glorious friendship. With more than the wisdom of the great Athenian teacher, He instructed His disciple band; with a thousandfold more of personal charm than Carlyle or Emerson, Christ, who spake as never man spake, wrought tirelessly for His little company.

He found the fishermen rude, cold and unlettered. He found them dull and low-flying, and He poured warmth and light about them, and lent fertility and ripeness to their every faculty. Partly by instruction, but chiefly by the might of a glorious love, He lifted them out of themselves and transformed the fisherman Peter into a great apostle, and led the untutored John toward the stature of a poet, mystic and seer. Then came the Last Supper, and Judas, followed by the conspirators, stooped for his kiss of treachery. Having loved His own, Jesus loved unto the end. To Him the thought that Judas was to be lost was an unbearable thought. He makes one more attempt! Again and again His infinite love wrestled with Judas' selfishness and rebellion! No quick words, that burn like lightning, leap from Christ's lips! No sentence falls like a club to crush Judas to the earth, as a big man brings a little one down by a single blow.

With infinite pity, with all the ingenuity of love, with tireless solicitude, Christ begins His work afresh. "Friend, wherefore art thou come?" Twice His hand was stretched out to draw the man back from the precipice, as He seeks to snatch Judas from the abyss that yawns. But all entreaties are in vain. What mystery is this, that man can set his will against His Maker's? Destiny is in these words, "I will not." Judas speaks or acts them, and so he went on toward the scrap heap of the universe.

Deliverance and salvation may be in God, but man can refuse them. Harvests are not alone in the sun! The sun falls on good soil and brings forth sheaves and shocks; the sun falls on thin sand, and the Sahara remains sand. On sunny, southern shores the sea rolls in, to feed the rich marsh-grasses and clothe the shores with vines and flowers, yet that self-same tidal wave rolls over the rocky point and the waters leave the rocks as they found them, clothed with bareness and with death. Thus an encircling sea of love encircled the disciple band! But if these sweet influences transformed the eleven, they were impotent to help the twelfth, named Judas. Therefore, in the *Inferno,* Dante makes the traitor stand apart, shunned by murderers, himself an abyss beyond all black depths. Having spoken as never man spake, having served and wrought as never man toiled, at last Christ, after three years of work for one of His disciples, fronted failure. The bitter, disappointed cry of the disciple is the disappointment of the Master, "What if all my work be in vain?"

Nations also have power to refuse the last pleadings of love and the influences of God's providence. Now and then history shows us an entire people rising up to say, "We will not." In retrospect, Southern historians tell us that in 1830 the South was in the position of control, and held far greater promise than the North, by reason of resources undeveloped and opportunities offered by events. In that hour blindness fell upon the people. The Huguenots in the South forgot Admiral Coligny, and their fathers' brave struggle for liberty. The sons of Albion, who had settled in Virginia, forgot the glories of the English Revolution, and the emancipation of serfs and peasants! Men with Swiss blood in their veins forgot the struggle of the cantons and the overthrow of despotism. The cotton gin increased the love of gold. That tool doubled the value of every acre of cotton land. It raised the price of every slave from $100 to $1,000. Avarice became universal. One day Lincoln was elected President. He thought slavery was wrong and should be ended. The South thought slavery was right, and should be expanded.

But from the day he was elected, Abraham Lincoln, that giant mentally as well as physically, began to plead with his Southern friends. He urged them to stop and consider; that if they were going wrong, time would correct their judgment; that if they were going right, time would not injure their prospects. He urged that the North and South had a common tradition, a common language, a common liberty, a common succession of Anglo-Saxon ideas; that the North and South could not separate themselves physically, nor build an impassable wall between. Afterwards Lincoln passed into a mood of depression. He began to fear lest his plea had failed. His face in that hour was more marred than any face of his time. So he makes his last plea of love: "My fellow-countrymen, I am loath to close. We are not enemies, but friends. We must not be enemies. Though passion may have strained, it must not break our bonds of affection. The mystic chords of memory, stretching from every battlefield and patriot grave to every living heart and hearthstone all over this broad land, will yet swell the chorus of the Union, when again touched, as they surely will be, by the better angels of our nature."

It was a noble plea, but "it was all in vain." Four years passed by, and lo, a battlefield a thousand miles in length; a wasted land; ruins where had been villages, cripples marching through every Northern and Southern city; black-robed women going up and down the land; an army of orphans robbed of their defenders. Oh, awful and mysterious gift—the gift of the free will that can refuse the plea of love and turn life into waste and desolation!

In the larger sense, the divine government over man, with all its myriad threads of influence, may be in vain. Man is not alone in the universe. He is a single thread, held in all the texture into which he has been woven! During these days, God seems near to men! As of old, so now, the heavens declare His glory. Even the scientists will not permit us to forget the nearness of the invisible Ruler and Guide. Witness that incident related by Sir Oliver Lodge! The scientist and a distinguished physician were driving together. "And do you, indeed, still believe in prayer?" asked the physician. "Do you believe it, right down to the ground? Does not God govern the world according to natural laws? How can He interrupt these laws to answer prayer? What is a man anyway? Only one of fifteen hundred million tiny insects?" Then the scientist took the physician to task. The reply was substantially, that he must begin to read the new books on science, that the old ones that were controlling his thought were now on the top shelf, forgotten and covered with dust. And this was the scope of his argument:

"Years ago you did not believe in the X-ray. If anyone had told you that there was a light that would make the body transparent, so that you could see the bones in your hand, and perhaps the needle broken off against the bone, you would have scoffed at the suggestion. But the X-ray was here, despite all these centuries of ignorance and unbelief. A few years ago, you did not believe in radium. You would have thought it unscientific to believe that the flame should not consume; that a substance does not burn itself up by its own blaze. Now, however, you believe in radium—the very thing that once you would have denied as irrational. Ten years ago, as a physician, you would have ridiculed the idea of influencing the human will by hypnotic suggestion. You would have said that it violates the sanctity of personality. Now, you recognise the principle, and as a surgeon working with your patients, you constantly practice it. You cannot explain by what physical or mental threads you influence men, but it is a fact, and these are facts that scientists must reckon with. Believing in these three things, during the last few years, you must remember that the X-ray, radium and mental suggestion had a therapeutic force, antedating your faith, and existing from the very beginning! And now, who are you, that you shall believe the less, but not the greater? Who are you, that you deny that God, also, by suggestion of truth, of beauty, of goodness, cannot control and govern men, and so answer prayer?" Then the two men parted. The next morning, in London, the scientist says he received a telegram containing these words: "Last night I said my prayers, for the first time in thirty years." And so the scientist led the physician into the faith and joy of his childhood!

Of a truth, God is once more round about us all. Again, He is nearer to us than our breathing. The sky above is a blue page written over with the tracery of His hand; the rocks beneath hold His footprints. It is God who makes work so sweet; it is God who sends man rest and sleep; it is God who fills the day with splendour; it is God who overflows the cup of night with majesty. It is His stroke that falls in the storm; it is His breath that sweeps away the clouds and mists. It is God who is the sum of all excellencies. Just as the flowers borrow the one its red, the other its blue, the other its violet or gold from the sunbeam that holds all, so the great ones of earth borrow their heroism, their love of liberty, their truth, their self-sacrifice, their every splendid virtue, from God. His love flows round about you as the ocean laves the base of some Gibraltar. His light, like the sun, lends beauty to your life. His every thought is medicinal, His sacred influences are curative, His spirit brings vitality and health. The angel of His Providence goes before you, to mark out your pathway, the angel of His mercy follows after you, to recover you from transgression; the angel of His love encamps on your right hand and on your left. With ceaseless solicitude He woos and pleads with you. This is His voice, "My son, give me thine heart." Your life is like a book; it is written by a human and a divine hand jointly. The pages are filled with the record of God's government over you. What, then, if the last page of your life history should hold these words, "It is all in vain"!

Consider that the patience of God, His interference in men's behalf and all His providential deliverances may also be in vain. Every man is unconsciously writing his autobiography. And what a book of life yours would make! If your career were told, verily, truth would be stranger than fiction. What critical hours once came upon you! What moments of destiny have been yours. Oft you have stood upon the very brink of a precipice, and a Divine Hand was stretched forth to draw you back. How thrilling the interferences of God in your youth! You can recall the year at school, when you passed under the ascendency of one whose whole influence was malign. For months that shadow darkened and eclipsed your days. In retrospect, you look upon that boon companion as attractive and fascinating, but tending toward evil. From him at last you broke away, but through and by what power and help you do not know! The path of your lives parted; he went one way, and came to inevitable destruction; you were led along another way, and escaped as from the snare of a fowler. But during all that epoch, when you were under the malign influence, the evil forces were eating into your life, cutting into character as decay cuts into fruit, as rust eats into steel, as a moth bores into a garment. Had that relation not been interrupted, the whole structure of your life would have come crashing down in ruins. But God entered the scene. An invisible hand with sword of flame, sundered the relation. An unseen angel delivered you, and led your steps into another path. Lo, now you stand forth in life, strong, surely founded, and buttressed by truth and justice. In that hour of deliverance what vows you made. You were swift to make pledges. Were you not swifter still to forget them?

Do you not recall that epoch when, through overwork, disease fell upon you? Do you remember the day when the pulse fluttered, and your heart was as weak as the flutter of a leaf? How physician and friend went about whispering, while none knew what the issue would be? In that hour, looking upward with fevered eye, did you not cry out, "God of my fathers! spare my life, and I will live for Thee! Every hour shall be spent in Thy service! Thine henceforth shall be health, gold and all gifts"? Oh, what a prayer was yours! Well, God heard your prayer. Stretching His hand down into the depths, He lifted you out and set your feet upon the rock. Have you kept your vows? Have all your gifts, and gold, and life, been used for Him? You know they have not. Shall all those marvelous interferences be in vain?

Some of you have been overwhelmed in a weak hour by some temptation of avarice, or stupidity, or passion. This overthrow was as sudden as if some wild beast had leaped out of a jungle and left you bleeding in the way. At last you have risen above the body, you have flung down the cup of flame, calling upon God for deliverance. Then the day of liberty came. But with strength of will have you lived by day and by night for your Deliverer as you promised and pledged? What perilous hours some of you have had in finance! What risk of bankruptcy! What moments of persecution! What losses and bereavements! God delivered you out of them all. Have you kept the vows you made in return? When Judas retraced his steps, lo, at every turn in the path some ghost rose up to torment him. Go back over your long life pathway. Live once more the great critical hours. Recall the nights when, like young Jacob, God's angel met you in the way, and you promised that you would give your life to Him. For the living angel now, only the spectre and the ghost remain. You have broken your vows, you have forgotten God's deliverance, you have repressed the nobler feelings. God stirred anew great deep convictions within you, but all these you have tried to choke down. A thousand times One whose form is like unto the Son of God entered your life, now warding off dangers, now exposing pitfalls, now planting flowers along your life's way; now sheltering you from sin's fierce heat, but the more God has given, the more selfish you have become. Thou rich man! thou hast become a Dead Sea into which all rivers run and from which no generous stream flows forth! Thou man of culture, with much knowledge thou hast overburdened thy life. Having received much, thou hast given little. In vain God has interfered, hoping still to recover you. Soon you will be at the end of the life pathway, and when the career is done, what if these words are written there: "Lo, it was all in vain"?

For multitudes, the closer and more intimate influences of God in man's behalf are exerted in vain. Great is the influence of God in nature and events. Marvellous the way in which God influences men through land and sea and sky. His truth breaks forth in the story of nations and of great men. What a voice is the voice of revelation through this divine Book! But God also deals with men in a more intimate way. For conscience has a voice and it can speak. A thousand books have been written to explain this voice, but the sum of them all is, that conscience is the whisper of God in the soul of man. It is as if the youth ever heard one bidding him remember the all-seeing eye, the all-hearing ear, and the books of judgment that record all deeds. For pain does not more certainly follow a wound than does conscience condemn a wrong. God hath not left Himself without a witness in any human heart. If so-called heathen peoples have no temple or teacher or book, day by day, and through all the rolling years, they do have the voice of conscience. Witness

Lucretius in his *De Rerum Natura.* "The evil doer needs no dungeon, no scourge, no executioner's sword. For conscience, that dread avenger, is ever with him." Witness the old Persian when the wild beasts leaped upon him and rent him, and his servants carried him home to die. He exclaimed, "I thank God that I have been rent by a beast, and not by the fangs of conscience."

And to every noble youth God speaks. In the hour of temptation, the voice whispers warning and alarm. In the hour of yielding and fall, conscience brings condemnation and stern punishment. If the youth persists and scoffs at everything that makes for love, conscience still pleads. But alas, the time will come when the conscience will be seared by sin as by a red-hot iron, until the youth loses his innocence, and maturity is contaminated, and old age becomes degradation and conscience is dead.

Yet, as long as there is the faintest whisper, there is hope. Oh, thou man, grown grey in thy refusals, listen! If thou dost catch but the tremor of the whispered note of reproof, then thank God; thank Him with tears running down the cheek that conscience is not dead, and that God still calls, that hope is still yours, that still there is room and opportunity. But, remember, that when conscience speaks to the Judas-like faculty in you, it is God speaking. Do not refuse. Remember that when Christ said to Judas, "Friend, wherefore art thou come?" the disciple said nothing. Judas did not say, "I will not." He simply said nothing. He did not refuse, he only postponed. He did not curse; he simply delayed. In refusing to commit himself to the right, he allied himself to wrong. If you turn away, today, having made no vow to God, having postponed your acceptance of His Son, having kept silence, you have chosen Judas' part, and all the warnings of conscience, all the pleas of the whisper of God, in the soul of man, will have been for naught. And when conscience speaks for the last time, this will be her word: "Lo, all my work has been in vain!"

It seems, therefore, that the issues of life and death hang upon the will. It is not enough that men should desire good, they must, with instant resolution, *choose* the good, and give themselves to it with entire abandon. It is often said that men are in danger of emotionalism in religion. People are urged not to act in haste. "Take plenty of time," friends whisper. When a man is thinking about committing a crime, "the second thought is the best thought." But when a man is thinking about doing right the second thought is treachery. Remember that the first thought of good is the only thought to be followed with instant decision and energy!

Life is a battle. Every day brings its test. No man is safe until he is carried to the cemetery. Evil surges round the soul, beating it with ever constant stroke. The way of instant resolution is the only way of safety. No counsel can be more foolish than the counsel for delay, postponement and consideration. In an hour like that of the Iroquois Theatre fire, it is the foolish man who says: "Consider. Wait for the second thought. Avoid precipitancy." The one duty of the moment is to make haste. Save yourself first, consider afterward.

You are on the great overland express. Some passing spark has kindled a flame on the bridge, and it is burned through. The locomotive goes down. Startled by the jerk, you spring to the door of the sleeper. The car hangs on the edge; the one duty is that of precipitancy. You must act,—act for your life. This is also the law of the soul. In those hours when God is brooding upon you, and the finer feelings rise, commit yourself. Turn to the man sitting beside you, and say: "For years I have been wrong. I am determined to do right." Speak to every friend you meet, announcing your decision. Give hostages to pride. Many and many a man might have been saved had he but acted with decision and energy.

There are men who have been gambling in secret; some of you have been tempted, and have yielded. You are standing upon the edge of a precipice; go forth tomorrow and build buttresses between you and evil. When a sentinel gives the word that the enemy is approaching, the regiment hastily throws up an earthwork, and sleeps behind defenses. You must take sides, and buttress yourself about and guard all the ledges and walls. This is the function of the Church. This is the philosophy of Christ's word: "If any man is ashamed of Me and of My word, of him will I be ashamed when I come into My kingdom." Do not be deceived; God is not mocked; you are coming to an hour of shame and peril. You think that you have some excuse for not walking in the band of Christ's disciples, for not carrying His banner. Do you think that if Jesus were in your place He would refuse and stand aloof as you have stood for years? All the little, flimsy excuses that you have been making for keeping out of His Church are as impotent as drifting leaves. You must choose. Why not now?

Swiftly the years come and go. Already some of you are approaching the end. Did you but know it, you are even now in sight of the homeland. Just as men trained to the sea perceive the smell of the soil in the air, before the shore comes in sight, so are the foretokens and intimations of the life beyond now being made clear. Already the air is full of voices, if only you had ears to hear. And yet, you are still in the winter of your discontent. Restlessness disturbs you; with fear and shrinking you draw back from the end. More and more you cling to the things called bonds and goods and houses, not knowing that soon these ambitions will explode like balloons, while the whole fabric dissolves. When it is too late, you will discover that these things that you have pursued are only for the support of the body, that the things of the soul alone are of real consequence!

In that hour, you will recall all the interferences of God in your behalf. What has your career been but a succession of overtures from the all-loving Father God? And are all these events to be in vain? What a father and mother you had! Are their graves to mean nothing to you? What teachers and what companions in life's way! What offices, and joys, and honours, and victories, God has sent you! Are all these to be in vain? What a succession of prophets and apostles and martyrs who have inspired and guided you! Is their work to come to naught? What means this voice, this still, small voice, that whispers and still whispers: "Behold, now is the accepted time; behold, now is the day of salvation." "My son, give me thine heart." Is this also to be of no avail?

Oh, I am loathe to close! For God and your soul are not enemies, but are friends. You must not be enemies. Though selfishness and sin have strained, they must not break the bonds of affection. In my vision I see the mystic chords of memory stretch from your heart and hearthstone and your mother's grave, to the arms of yonder Cross that stands on Calvary. Surely the chords will give forth music of the Christian life when the angels of God and your better nature touch the strings. Do not go out into the night undecided, as Judas did, for if you do, then all has been in vain. That would mean that the harvest is past, the summer ended, and your soul not saved!

III

MESSENGERS AT THE GATE

"And the Lord God of their fathers sent to them by his messengers."—II CHRON. xxxvi: 15.

NEWMAN says, "there are two supreme and self-evident realities in the universe,"—God, above the stars, and man below, asking what is going on beyond those star-fires. From time to time man thinks that he sees signals hung out from the battlements, and in his vision hours, he makes answer thereto. This interchange of signals forms the basis of religion. When God speaks unto men it is inspiration and guidance. When man speaks unto God it is prayer and worship. What God once did for Moses and Paul, He still does for modern merchants and husbandmen.

Not that the messengers always speak with human voices, for His is a rich and varied language. Now He puts Right upon the scaffold and Wrong upon the throne, and bids men choose between them. Now He sends the Angel of Memory to freshen ideals grown dim, and so disturbs man's contentment. Now He sends the anniversary of some rich and thrilling yesterday, to unseal life's secret springs.

He spoke to David through a stern prophet, who dragged the guilty king before the judgment seat.

He spoke to Solomon through Fear, a great and awful figure, "treading on the leaves of yester-year." He came to Peter through the common things of life—busy with the day's work at his fishing nets, and called the fisherman to a new career. Every day some messenger stands knocking at the door of man's soul, bringing overtures from beyond.

The soul is an imperial palace with many and rich rooms. Intellect is a vast entrance hall; memory is a library filled with treasures; imagination is a gallery with portraits of heroes, angels or seraphs; conscience has her judgment seat, and from time to time messengers stand at the door. Sometimes they thunder at the threshold, and sometimes they whisper at the windows. After accomplishing his murderous will upon the sleeping Duncan, Macbeth went into his wife's room, closed the door and turned the key. It was midnight. The stars were out, and not a leaf was stirring. In that stillness, guilty Macbeth thought he could hear even the heartbeat of the princess. Macbeth thought he heard steps in the hall and whisperings at the door. One voice said, "Sleep no more. Macbeth hath murdered sleep!" Months passed over the palace while the king guarded his black secret. But Memory kept the face of the dead ever before him. Conscience knew, and even at the banquet Macbeth saw the dead man appear at the threshold. Like Jacob, the guilty king had met God's messenger in life's way. For evermore he was to hear in the night the footfall of the unseen pursuer, for Nemesis was upon his track.

Oh, it is a thrilling journey that the soul makes across the continent of the years, and for man's safety and recovery oft messengers are in the way. Many centuries ago Jacob met certain messengers in life's highway. That youth had deceived his father, robbed his brother, betrayed conscience, and now Jacob was overtaken by retribution. Fleeing from the anger of Esau and the indignation of Isaac, the youth became a fugitive from justice. Alone in the desert, Jacob, the youth, was not alone. The fear that a troop of armed men might any moment overtake him shook Jacob until he was like unto a reed shaken in the wind. At sunset he prayed God that darkness might come and hide him from Esau's vengeance. When the night fell and he was alone in the desert, the stars came out and blazed—and blazed, always the stars, two by two, blazing and still blazing, and refusing to let him sleep. Often, in the desert, he stopped his flight and fell upon his knees to confess his sin, to weep over his deceit and to pray God for pity and pardon. Exhausted, he fell back into troubled slumber, only to see the star on the horizon lengthen into a long beam of light—and then into a ladder, that sloped upward toward God's throne. In his dream he saw the angels descending to bring good cheer, and ascending to bear his penitence up to God. In that moment hope began to stir in his heart—hope that black and false as he was, God might still pardon a fugitive and an exile, and help him redeem his past and build a better future.

How human and real this chapter in the story of

a man's soul! It might almost be a page torn out of your own biography—so unaffected, artless and moving is this story. Nor need any man in this twentieth century think that if visions once came to Jacob in the morning of history, that the era when God sends messengers has passed forever. No life is so isolated, no talent so obscure, no cabin so remote but God girds the worker for his task and expects His servant to play a man's part. It is only in the river that the drop melts and loses its individuality. In that human stream flowing along Broadway every individual is a separate drop that cannot coalesce with its fellows. Every soul is as separate as a star that dwells a million miles apart from its nearest fellow. Your autobiography is filled with thrilling events, epoch-making moments, when you met the messengers divine in the way. Just because you are a man, out on the frontier line, a man full of red blood tingling with ambition, struggling with temptation, oft staggering with burdens, a man having in your hand the destiny of others, because a little pilgrim band is following you as leader, your journey along life's way is a thrilling drama, that fully justifies the entrance of the messengers of God into the earthly scene.

Memory is a messenger at the gate of man's soul. To the pilgrim in life's way comes the angel of memory. Man lives a threefold life called yesterday, today and tomorrow. All the yesterdays are his through memory, the tomorrows through hope, while today is presided over by reason. Hours come to us all, when memory approaches bearing in her arms the sheaves of yesteryear.

Then she talks to us as with a familiar friend. While the soul is busy here and there, suddenly Memory waves her wand, and summons Lady Macbeth to her secret tribunal. From this subpœna there is no appeal. The guilty queen is reluctant and rebellious, but Memory will not take "No." She drags the beautiful woman upon the stage. Suddenly the curtain is rung up, the play begins, and the centre of the tragedy is always herself. Now Lady Macbeth is welcoming Duncan to the castle, now she is sharpening the dagger for her husband's hands, now she is stopping up all the springs of mercy, now she is filling him with hatred from top to toe. Scene by scene, the tragedy is enacted and re-enacted, until every figure is etched in fire. Oft the guilty queen tries to shut out the scene by closing the eyes, but lo, conscience touches the eyelids and makes them transparent. Oft she tries to rise and flee the play, but her feet are lead! Full oft she journeys to other and different scenes, but lo, all the scenery of that tragic drama is carried about in her own soul, like a traveling company of players, who carry their scenery with them. No closet nor cell in the castle so remote, no wall so thick, but that when she listens, the footfall of Memory is heard approaching!

Some men's sins go beforehand unto judgment, and some sins follow after, under the guidance of Memory. As witnesses they come late to furnish testimony against the transgressor, and convict him of his crime. And that which was unique and tragic, in that old castle, holds true of every man's life. What an illuminated missal and illustrated volume is Memory! Memory is like a book that lies upon your lap! Swiftly the scenes change as you turn the pages! Now you are looking upon the old house where you were born. Now upon the faces of your mates on the old playground, now upon the forest where in October days you went with shouts for fruit and ripened nuts! Now you behold the face of companions who long ago passed away; now you hear your mother's voice, and with her walk the old familiar paths, and fulfil the dear old tasks. The thought that all those scenes are gone, and gone forever, dims your eyes and brings a lump into your throat. What magic is in the voice of this messenger, named Memory! What sacred ministry is hers, for rebuke, correction, and instruction in righteousness! Uncover thine head, for the place where thou standest is holy ground. Meeting Memory thou hast met God's angel in life's way.

Journeying along life's way, the pilgrim meets another angel in the highway, and the name of that messenger is Fear. The wise king said "the fear of the Lord is the beginning of wisdom." When man opens the book of life, and reads the first paragraph, he reads words penned by Fear, but when man comes to the last chapter of the book of life he finds that the love of God is the end of wisdom, and her crown. Long time stands between the seed and with its fruit of the date palm, but the seed is the important thing; and that seed of fear may, after long time, ripen into the fruit of obedience and loyalty. Fear sits in the window of a man's soul, and hears afar off the approach of iron feet. Fear announces the coming of an armed troop. Fear looks toward the horizon when the first red beam of day shoots up, and prophesies storm clouds, earthquakes, the overthrow of houses and the fall of the city. The wicked flee when no man pursueth, for the sound of a quivering leaf shall chase him. The coward dies a thousand deaths, yet still lives on. Charles Dickens brings the fugitive to a garret in a deserted house. The room is an attic, the window broken, the scene squalid, the rafters thick with spiders' webs. Never was a hiding place more secure, or better chosen. Suddenly a noise is heard. It is a mouse at a knothole in the floor. Fear enlarges the tiny eyes until they become big as the eyes of a policeman. The fugitive starts up in terror. The muscles standing out like whipcords. Cold sweat streams from his face. Of what is the fugitive afraid? What vague and awful figure, spectre-like, is pursuing this guilty man? There is a disease of the tongue that sets the papillæ thrilling with the silliest forms of pleasure and exquisite delight, to be followed a moment later with pains that pierce like swords, for Nature has turned upon herself in this diseased condition. Thus sin has so outraged this fugitive's soul that Fear has become his pursuer and Conscience his executioner, while Remorse is a cord that chokes the throat. The penalty of sin is not public exposure. The youth who trembles at the thought of discovery through his employer will find a terror beyond that. Retribution is not imposed by jailors. Hell is not something to come, in far-off realms! Milton speaks for all men—"myself am hell."

Over in a city of Pennsylvania, old men still tell the story of the Molly Maguire murders. A brave detective joined the secret society under an assumed name. He became its secretary, kept the records of all meetings, and sent daily transcripts of all plans for crime unto the officials. At last the time came for justice and penalty. The leaders were brought to trial. The court room was crowded with several hundred men, each one of whom felt that his own relation to the crimes were quite unknown and unexpected. At last the moment struck. The prosecuting attorney called the name of Captain McParlan. The onlookers smiled. Not one of them had ever heard of James McParlan. Suddenly a man stepped forward, and took his place upon the witness stand, saying, "I am James McParlan!" Lo, he was their own secretary! He held their secrets. He knew not only their names, but had kept the records of their crimes. For thirty seconds that room held but one heart, and that heart did not beat nor breathe! Then one low, gurgling sob swept over that courtroom. Full fifty men broke into one muffled curse. A moment later more than fifty men were plunging through windows and doors in panic as they fled from justice and penalty. That was perhaps the most thrilling moment in the history of American crime! Of necessity, Fear casts its shadow on before. It is the twilight going before the advancing darkness and night. Fear is the thunderbolt leaping out of a cloud big with retribution. It's voice whispers, "Whatsoever a man soweth, that shall he reap." For Fear is a God-sent messenger! Therefore the wise man said, "The fear of the Lord is the beginning of wisdom." It warns man to keep God's commandments, for this is indeed "the whole duty of man."

Another messenger of God is the angel of Reverence that comes to touch man's soul with the sense of awe. For Reverence lies at the very heart of all that is noblest in man. If Moses' face shone without, it was because that majestic soul had stood before the quaking mount, and knelt before the bush blazing with the presence of God. Reverence is the upward look that lifts the soul to divine levels. For the youth who finds nothing in the universe to admire, there is nothing left to fear. To him every evil thing has already happened! The house of his soul is already ruined! Milton understood. The poet made Lucifer revolt against the sense of awe and reverence. This proud angel desired no intellect superior to his own, denied there could be a throne, before which he must bow. Lucifer was willing to look down upon his inferiors, but unwilling to look up toward the throne where dwelt infinite Wisdom and Love! When reverence goes, all nobility falls. The vulgarity, the sordidness, the meanness of some modern literature and art is explained by this revolt against reverence. Coleridge's hymn at Chamonix was born of a poet who was great enough to prostrate himself in an hour when the white snows of Mont Blanc became altars, when the white clouds became prayers, and all the falling of the waterfalls and the cry of the eagles were transmuted into hymns of praise, rising to the throne of the Unseen God. Man's soul descends to the level of the beast, in the hour when it loses the sense of splendour and sanctity that haunts midnight and midday. Take reverence and awe out of the soul, and this universe all fretted with golden fires becomes a mere assembly of pestilential vapours. It is the sense of reverence that lends dignity and allurement to the battlefields of liberty, to the historic abbeys and memorials of the great, and to the tombs where heroes sleep. What thoughtful man can stand in that little garret in Stockbridge, where Jonathan Edwards wrote the greatest philosophical book of his century, *The Freedom of the Will,* without being conscious of reverence that refreshens the will and strengthens every purpose? What is it that casts the spell of silence and mystery upon the soul when we stand in the little house where Shakespeare was born? That which exalts the traveler, and lifts his being into a rapture of passionate delight as he walks the streets of Florence, is not its palaces, its galleries, its towers and domes; that which strikes the soul through with quivering delight is the sense of reverence and awe, born of the haunting presences of the martyred Savonarola, the divine Dante and the lofty, dedicated soul of Michael Angelo. Your dead have turned certain rooms in your homes into shrines of awe and chapels of veneration. Thither came the angels of God to release one you loved! Therefore you can never cross the threshold of that room without knowing that with altered eyes you look upon an altered world. Uncover thine head, for behold thou hast met God's angel in the way! Whatsoever that angel saith, do it!

God sends another messenger to man, and the name of that angel is Conscience. Other messengers are royal—this one is divine. Intellect chooses a course for the ship, constructive genius assembles the great cargo, but Conscience holds the compass, and steers by the eternal stars. God hath not left Himself without a witness concerning things that are wrong and right. Man is like a little child on the nether rim of a vast continent, and left to go alone into the wilderness, across the desert, over river and mountain; and man would have fallen by the way, had not certain angels encamped upon his right hand, and his left. In a moral universe no pilgrim can be permitted to do wrong, without warning of the peril thereof. When Joseph's brethren had sold their brother into slavery, God sent forth Conscience as a messenger to find them walking in the fields. Often had they promised one another never to speak Joseph's name, and yet the question would keep coming up: Is there danger of our father's discovering the crime we have wrought upon our brother? Even in their dreams they heard the crack of the slave-driver's whip, falling upon the innocent flesh of their own kinsman. Oft at midnight they shook with fear. There is a story of a traveler on the desert, who overtook a merchant named Ibycus. Inflamed by avarice, and suspecting that the traveler's rags were to create the impression of poverty, the youth slew the pilgrim and robbed him of the gems. As he was burying the body in the sand the traveler chanced to look up, and saw two wild fowl passing through the sky, on their way toward northern lakes, but the murderer gave the cranes only a passing thought. Going into the city, the youth sold the gems and bought his way to office and lands. Long afterward, one day, the slayer was watching the sports at the annual Olympic games. It was autumn. Suddenly from the sky he heard the cry of the wild fowl and, looking up, saw two cranes, flying southward. Springing from his seat, the man stretched upward his arms and cried out, "The cranes of Ibycus! The cranes of Ibycus!" Soon the story came to the ears of a friend of the diamond merchant who had disappeared. Why had Ibycus never returned? How did this man know his name? The thread soon drew a garment, and lo, the garment drew in the dead man's body. One day the slayer stood before the judge, told the whole story, and asked for punishment. He said he hungered for punishment, as the pilgrim for water! Such power hath Conscience to touch natural objects, and at the cock's crow, makes Peter weep! As the sun goes down in the afternoon, makes Saul shake with terror! At the sound of a trumpet calling the advance, makes David choke with fear; at the flight of two wild cranes in the air shakes that Greek with terror. Memory and Conscience forget nothing! Deeds do not die. Sins are seeds which by and by will bring a harvest of penalty. Every man must give an account of every secret thing unto God!

Another messenger stands at the gates of man's

soul, with face most beautiful and name of Love! Beholding the rusty hinges of the door, he stands at the threshold and knocks. He wears no black robes of penalty, waves no flaming sword of Conscience, brings no fetters forged by Fear. He stretches out his hands to shield and bless. For Him laws are not hurtling thunderbolts. For Him, laws are warnings, and safeguards sent to ignorant and foolish men. Unto each soul he whispers, "Thou art mine! Thou hast been mine from the beginning at thy cradle!" The gifts he brings are gifts of forgiveness, peace, and redemption from the past. All he asks is acceptance of the treasure he holds in his hands. Ever Love whispers: "The past is yours, in memory; the future also, through hope. This throbbing, present moment also is thine! Therefore rise up and follow me."

Oh, all ye young hearts! Soon we will go the way of all the earth. What you do, do quickly. The Stranger at the door met Nicodemus only once. Once only He made overtures of friendship to the Samaritan woman. Once He spake to the young ruler, and once only the ruler went away never to return! Unto every one of you, today, signals have been hanged out. Lo, messengers are here! Staying your steps today for one moment! Rise ere it be too late! What strong man but remembers an hour of peril when certain destruction impended, and when you cried to your father's God, and deliverance came! Surely you dare not affirm that God's angels in the way have never met you! What woman can but recall certain golden hours when the clouds were filled with light, and the way became plain! Down in your heart you know that in that hour you met God's angel in the way. What youth, choosing paths of pleasure and passion has not awakened to utter exhaustion and nausea, and cried out in disgust. There in fear and remorse you met angels in life's way. And now, again, unseen messengers are at the gate! They wait your answer! Do not delay! Harden not your hearts! Surrender the will! Dedicate your talents, realising that what you do determines character and fixes destiny! The hour is big with destiny! What answer will you give to the stranger standing at the door? The mere refusal to decide is an answer in itself! Therefore rise up, forsake all, and follow the Lord of life—the Master of destiny!

IV

HOURS WHEN MEN GO DOWN

"And Esau came in from the field. . . . And Esau said to Jacob, Feed me, I pray thee, with that same red pottage; for I am faint: And Jacob said, Sell me this day thy birthright. And Esau said, Behold, I am at the point to die; and what profit shall this birthright be to me? . . . and he sold his birthright unto Jacob."—GEN. XXV: 29-33.

THE ancient, poet-king is not a favourite of our generation, but the old Hebrews looked upon David as the ideal of a minstrel hero—their Hebrew Homer. The spell he cast upon his generation is described thus: "He seemed as an angel of God." From our viewpoint, David's fame rests upon his work as a reformer, a man who put down the revolt of the old native stock, ended the era of civil war, and started the people along lines of commerce and industry. Had he died during his forties, David's era would have been the golden age in Hebrew history. But, grown prosperous, he relaxed his moral muscles, and temptations came in like a flood. A goodly vineyard may be destroyed slowly through neglect, and its gradual processes; it may be destroyed swiftly by lifting an axe upon the vines. By one hour of neglect, David, like a keeper who slept at the gate of the castle, let his enemies in, and the whole structure of his life came crashing down. So grievous were the mistake and sin that he found no place of repentance, though he sought it long with tears. The king was untrue to his people, the shepherd betrayed his flock, the soldier was false to the chivalry of arms. From that hour he became the target toward which misfortune and trouble pointed all their venomed shafts.

The essence of a hundred ordinary tragedies, like those of Sophocles and Shakespeare, are swept into David's single career. The shepherd boy begins in the fields, like one of the Horatii, became the champion against Goliath, and was the idol of the people. As Hamlet avoided the king's poison, so David escaped Saul's javelin. As Macbeth, ever ambitious, went through slaughter to a throne, so David went through blood toward his happiness. As King Lear reaped sorrow from sin, going from his palace into the snow and pitiless storm, so David, in his old age, fled from his capital, and through Absalom discovered that "sharper than a serpent's tooth is a thankless child." As Queen Elizabeth planned the execution of Queen Mary, and made Davidson her scapegoat, so David used Joab as his instrument, and later would have made the soldier responsible for his own crime. Take it all in all, this is one of the biggest canvases ever spread, and has more dark and light, more crimson and black, than any tragedy in Shakespeare. Yet so strangely overruled was David's sin, that his psalm of repentance has been for centuries a spring of purity. Sobbing over its pages, Augustine found hope, and Thomas à Kempis peace. It was the Psalms that were best loved by John Bunyan, as they have been of many of the greatest saints and noblest heroes of history. How does a sin, like a bow, spring the soul back toward righteousness and God? No man knows, nor shall know, until we discover why the blackest sloughs grow white lilies.

The extremes of life strained David's strength to the uttermost. Startling changes and sudden contrasts test men, and sometimes break them down. The wise physician guards the invalid against the trying days of February, when one day the south wind blows softly and the next day the north wind blows sharply and the mercury falls thirty degrees below freezing point. Heat iron red-hot, then plunge it into ice-water, and soon the extremes will make the atoms lose their grip. Molten ruby glass must be guarded, for a drop of cold water will feather the crimson glass, and shiver it. The old science talked about the fire-bellows melting rocks, and the ice-ploughs smoothing them, and brought the two extremes close together. The new science tells us that a million years stood between the era of fiery heat and the glacial epoch, and that there were no sharp extremes. But, now and then, there is a David in whom all the extremes, strength and weakness, gold and crusts, palace and hut, hilltop and valley, are in close juxtaposition. Witness Job, strained, tested and tempered, by extremes. Now he has palace, children, a troop of friends, herds, flocks; now the palace falls, through an earthquake, his children are dead, his gold takes wings, his herds disappear, health gives way, friends desert, his wife scoffs, and his Gethsemane hour is very bitter. The Satan of the drama was sure that the extremes would break Job down, and that his career would end with curses, rebellion and wickedness.

Witness many men whom you have known in this great city. The youth came up hither unknown and friendless. Personal charm opened golden doors. Soon he sends his plans out like merchant ships, carrying rich cargoes. Office, honours, prosperity—all are his. Then reverses come. Life's summer day ends with a black storm, clouds are piled mountain high, and the whole earth reels under the shock. When the clouds part, the man is peeled and stripped. Naked he entered into life, and naked he goes out. Oh, these reverses of prosperous men! Today fame, tomorrow obscurity. Today riches, tomorrow the treasures have taken wings and fled away! Today, loved ones, tomorrow, the silent house and the voice that is still. Today, a giant's strength, tomorrow, the grasshopper become a burden. Unforeseen, these extremes and reverses are inevitable as well as sudden. The Lord's hand lifteth men up, and it is His will that casteth men down. Suddenly, David went from his father's flocks to the king's palace, from obscurity to the position of place; from neglect, to the crowds that shouted when he appeared on the streets. Soon the spiced wine went to his head. Dizzy, he saw men as streets walking. Becoming vain, and selfish, his moral distinctions were blurred. He lost his simplicity of soul, and its loss was fatal. Stumbling, he plunged into the abyss of infamy and crime. Oh, it was a black fall! Not one hideous line must be softened nor one black spot concealed. The explanation is in life's extremes, for he who climbs high has the farther to fall, and is the more hurt when he hits the bottom of the abyss.

Temptations overtook the poet-king in unguarded moments. There is a proverb among ship captains that no anchor chain is stronger than its weakest link. Man's strength also is no greater than his weakest hour. There are epochs and moods when the intellect is struck through with light, when moral distinctions are so clear, when virtue is so beautiful, and self-sacrifice and truth so alluring, that the soul turns away from temptation and sin as the nostril and the eye turn from the mire and filth. Hours of publicity come, when the employer, the politician, the citizen, are centers of scrutiny, and, standing in the limelight, the man is on his mettle, and shows himself at his best. If life were a stage, and you were an actor, and all the people were in the mood to applaud noble deeds and to hiss selfish ones, you would never go astray. Life's perilous hours are the quiet hours—hours of rest, relaxation and solitude. At these moments Satan, like an angel of light, plans his attacks. The story of the decisive battles of the world indicates that the strongest side of a fortress is the weakest side, and there the enemy gains entrance.

Read the history of the capture of Quebec. One side of the fortress is a precipice, and that was left to take care of itself; the other three sides were exposed, and there Montcalm massed his forces for defense. Meanwhile, Wolfe knew that the precipice was the place to be attacked. Apparently, Wolfe was trying to force an entrance on the three dangerous sides, yet when the day dawned Montcalm discovered that a regiment of soldiers had scaled the precipice and were pouring hot shot into his rear. And so the apparently impregnable fortress fell. Thus men do not go down on the side where they are weakest; they are attacked on the side where they are strongest and apparently need least defense. Men like Robert Burns have nearly always been destroyed through temptations called godlike. Had evil approached the poet and tempted him to cruelty, lies, theft, treason, he would have scoffed at the allurements, and trampled them underfoot like the scorpion and the serpent. But when the men of the village drew Burns into a little inn, and he saw how sodden were their days, how cheerless their nights, how hungry they were for a little laughter and a little song, then, in his desire to please and make beautiful their hours, he poured out the cup of his genius, and often in a desire to give pleasure that was in itself a laudable ambition, he went down to base men's level, and mixed one evil drop in the honeyed cup. His drinking songs spread evil like a contagion, and so Burns' soul was spoiled and captured on the side where he was noblest.

That is why many of the promising men of every generation wreck their careers. The wasp chooses the largest and most glorious peach, and there stings the skin, and deposits the egg, and the worm goes to the heart of the luscious fruit. Satan seems to pass by selfish men, skinny souls and little, narrow intellects. Misers are seldom drunkards. Avaricious men do not love splendour, finery or show. The devil doesn't have to worry himself over Mr. Skinflint or Mr. Hard Scrabble. Satan knows that they are so mean that they will ruin their own souls without any external help. When heredity gives Aaron Burr the intellect of Jonathan Edwards, then, conscious of his mental superiority, the Spirit of Evil sends ambition to attack Aaron Burr, and the attack is made on the side where Burr is strongest, namely, his intellectual side. Ambition whispers that he is superior, and ought to outrank Hamilton and Jefferson and Adams, and when the country will not give him supremacy ambition whispers that he can go into the Southwest, and out of Mexico found a greater country. There fell Aaron Burr. Every man has the weakness of his strongest faculty. It is not the silent man that is tempted through over-speech; it is the man who has the art of putting things, who, in a mood of anger, sends out words that are like poisoned daggers that inflict injuries in one moment that a lifetime of struggle could not repair. Who shall measure the danger of these lawless hours when the sentinel sleeps and the City of Mansoul is exposed to peril? David was taken off guard. He was like the keeper of the castle, who thought no peril was near, unto whom came the gipsy girl, bringing cakes and wine, to overcome the youth who was stronger than Goliath, and, when his senses are stolen away, lo, the gipsy leads in the enemy's troop, and the champion of the army wakens from his stupor to find the castle in flames and his treasures gone. Oh, all ye young hearts, guard against your weaker hours. The vacation moment brings peril with its relaxation. The Saturday night, when the hours are all your own, and you are alone in the great city, and no eyes are upon you, and you seem lost, like a drop in a river, then watch and pray, lest ye enter into temptation, and the City of Mansoul be spoiled of its beauty and its divine treasure.

Superior natures, gifted men, a king like David, are tempted to believe that things are right for the sons of genius that would be wrong for ordinary men. In every age, gifted poets like David, gifted soldiers and men of genius, artists and orators, have claimed exemption from ordinary rules. In his history of the Renaissance, John Addington Symonds apologises for Andrea del Sarto's tragedy and Raphael's sins by saying: "We must remember that these artists are not to be judged like ordinary men." That was Byron's plea; he was a man of genius, and did not propose to submit himself to laws that were quite proper for peasants and clodhoppers. That was Wagner's plea, for when public opinion in Münich and Paris criticised him for cruelty, and neglect, to those whom he should have loved, he tossed off the moral obligations jauntily and haughtily by saying: "Am I not to have a little pleasure myself in hours when I am giving pleasure to the whole world through my genius?"

That, too, is the excuse of the industrial king, who lords it over his workmen, counting himself to be superior stuff, and this poet-king, who ruled by "divine right." The people cheered David in the streets, the women praised him, the children scattered flowers in his path, his will was law, and what he wanted he must have. An under-officer like Uriah had no rights that the king was bound to respect. Under-soldiers were clay, and the prince in the palace was marble and gold, and these distinctions must be observed. Let Uriah lose all, if King David but gain pleasure for a passing moment. And so David ruthlessly plucked the red rose out of poor Uriah's hand, and wore the flower for a day upon his own breast. But power brings peril. Privilege often breaks down the strongest. There is one argument against autocracy political, or autocracy industrial, that is sufficient—namely, the egotism and arrogance that are called out in even the best men by the sense of absolute power.

Witness the Stuarts. They ruled by what they called "divine right," and looked down from an infinite remove upon the common heard. Yet none of them, first to last, had brains enough to have earned five pounds a month. Their ability would have hardly warranted a man in hiring them as stable boys. All left a little slime on almost everything they ever touched. But for insufferable arrogance, colossal egotism, vapid impertinence, commend us to the letters and words of these enthroned nothings, these gilded ciphers, and perfumed humbugs. But you could hardly expect otherwise. When the Stuarts had absolute power, the corollary was that they had more power than other men because they had a different quality of soul from other men. Now and then the same spirit appears among the industrial kings. Occasionally a man who has charge of thousands of workmen grows despotic, tyrannical. Here is the industrial despot who sets himself against the right of working people to have a union. As he has many plants, he closes the one where the men belong to the union. At Martin's Ferry, the autocrat of industrial power found that about one-tenth of the men were unionised. He shut the works, kept them closed for twelve months, and nearly starved to death three or four thousand families. Personally, you and your friend may have such a love of independence that you do not want to surrender your liberty to a union, but the moment that unionised capital in some Martin's Ferry said to us, "You shall not do this, or you shall not do that," that moment, to assert our liberty, we would straightway unionise ourselves. Growing bitter, therefore, at the end of a year, the nine-tenths that never had belonged to the union, began to seethe like a pot, and when one found an anarchistic paper heaped up on the newsstand, the answer was eight hundred copies of that nihilistic sheet were being distributed in the town. One act of tyranny by that employer bred war and anarchy. Insufferable arrogance and the autocratic power of a unionised capitalist, who thought himself exempt from all ordinary laws, and superior to the every-day principles of American liberty threatened the prosperity of the whole region! One selfish industrial tyrant yonder can sow dragons' teeth for American society. This evil influence will reappear in pillage, arson, treason, and industrial warfare.

All sins are huge blunders, and every sin is big with its own penalty. Unto David, Satan came as an angel of light, and a hideous hog of vice was clothed like a beautiful angel of virtue. Strange the hypnotic power of sin, that can charm men, and dazzle their senses. Through these specious arguments, war that is nothing but murder, and legalised brigandage, becomes a means of securing the survival of the fittest. Drunkenness and passion are set forth as methods of doing away with the unfit. Slowly honesty is transformed into policy. Righteousness becomes mere expediency, until men are beasts of the field, and the strongest cattle horn away the weak ones, and secure the fodder. The end is that the cunning, the subtle, and the trickster flourish like the green bay tree, and live on life's good things, while patriots and heroes starve or go to the stake. Under this delusion David slew Uriah, but embraced, not an angel of happiness, but a demon that put a knife through his heart. The sin was a worm, boring at the heart of the tree, and one day the great tree, strong without, but rotten within, came crashing to the earth.

Satan pays foolish boys for their crimes, with counterfeit money, and then jeers at their anguish. After Jefferson Davis fled from Richmond, three wagons, loaded with Confederate paper money, were captured on the edge of the mountains. Davis worked the printing presses until they broke down. With amazement the handful of Union soldiers gazed at bills, piled up like bales of cotton. Being cold and cheerless, the Union boys pitched quoits that night for stakes of Confederate money. They played for $100,000 a game—in Confederate money. The next morning, one soldier boy bought a grey mule for a quarter of a million of dollars, and paid another $100,000 to have a shoe put on. Meanwhile these soldiers, rich in bales of money, were hungry and cold and houseless. One never sees a youth stretching out his hand toward these midnight pleasures, and taking gluttony and drunkenness into his bosom, without saying, " Satan is paying another boy off with lying money."

All these stock-jobbers, industrial deceivers and men who degrade their fellows are being deluded with counterfeit pleasures. Meanwhile, God is not mocked. Whatsoever a man soweth, that, in kind and in quality, he shall reap. For men cannot escape from the nature of things. Law entraps the transgressor. Conscience and memory are always with the wrong-doer. God also encamps on David's right hand and on his left, and makes his days to be remorse, and his nights misery. When Booth assassinated Lincoln, he locked the door of the box, had friends in the alley, a horse that was saddled, and everything sure. Booth had guarded against everything excepting God, and his country's flag. So, after Booth shot the President, the spur on his boot became entangled in the crimson bars of the flag in the President's box, throwing the assassin heavily to the floor, broke his ankle, and the flag stained with our father's blood, brought the assassin down and set him front to front with justice and penalty. For the nature of things is round about us, and there is no escape for David in the olden time, or for any transgressor today.

If we had only nature and law and science and memory and conscience, and the approaching judgment day, we should be of all men most miserable. But when Absalom rebelled against David, the father's heart turned in love toward the wicked son. In these days, when we are recalling everything that had to do with Abraham Lincoln, let me remind you of an incident in his life, that will explain the all-forgiving love of God. One day a telegram reached the White House, saying that Lee was about to surrender. That night Lincoln quietly left Washington and made his way to the front. And when the surrender came and the rebellion was over, and the officers were planning the entrance to Richmond, Lincoln waved aside all suggestions of a triumphal procession. This must be no Roman conqueror, moving along the Appian Way. There must be no chariots, no chargers, no bands of music. So, alone again, Lincoln entered Richmond. It was the strangest triumphal entrance in the annals of time. The sunshine fell on the Southern capital, but Lincoln seemed very tired as he started up the street. The Southerners had no greeting, their curtains were down. The President was alone. Slowly he walked. His head was on his breast. He seemed very sad. His steps were heavy. The slaves were in the alleys and in the side streets, and they wished to greet him, but were afraid. They met him on their knees, praying and sobbing and singing, but in low tones. On and on the worn, weary, broken President walked toward the house that was the capital of the Confederacy.

When he entered Davis' room, the President waved his two officers back. One of them, after a while, not understanding the silence, looked in. What strange victory in this President! What mystery in his triumph! Mr. Lincoln's head is down on Jefferson Davis' desk. His head is in his hands. The President is sobbing—weeping for the desolation of his beloved South, weeping for Rachel and her children, and he cannot be comforted, weeping for the brave Southern boys who will never come home, and perchance whispering to himself, "How often would I have gathered thee as a hen gathereth her chickens under her wings, and ye would not." We were not enemies, we were friends, but lo, ye would be enemies." And because this weary, broken man is staggering under his weight, and cannot be comforted, the great God took him home, and gathered him unto Himself, where the day dawned and the shadows fled away. And David the king, going up toward his palace, sobs, "Oh, Absalom, my son, Absalom, my son, my son! Would God I had died for thee, oh, Absalom, my son, my son!" Lo, we are Absalom, and this is the King of Time and of Eternity, abroad in the night on His mission of recovery, to bring us in out of the far off frontier, and the battle lines of sin, to heal our wounds, to forgive our transgressions, to cleanse away our iniquities.

V

THE BLEEDING VINE

"And, behold, a woman in the city, which was a sinner, when she knew that Jesus sat at meat in the Pharisee's house, brought an alabaster box of ointment, and stood at his feet behind him, weeping, and began to wash his feet with tears, and did wipe them with the hairs of her head, and kissed his feet and anointed them with the ointment. . . . And he said to the woman, Thy faith hath saved thee; go in peace."—LUKE vii: 38, 39, 50.

AS an apology for the slenderness of his book of reminiscences, the Beloved Disciple, with oriental imagery, said, if all the deeds and words of Jesus had been preserved the whole world could not contain the books that would be written. John means that if one sermon on the Mount was recorded, hundreds were never reported; that if a few brilliant parables, like the story of the Lost Coin, the Lost Sheep and the Lost Son, were written out, thousands of parables existed only in the memory of the eager hearers; and that if some wonder deeds of mercy were described in the Memorabilia of the Master, that other thousands were known only to the recipients of His kindness. But it could not have been otherwise. Consider the fertility of the intellect of Jesus! His mind blazed like a star, glowing and sparkling with ten thousand brilliant effects.

His genius was a rich garden, putting forth fruit and flowers in every nook and corner, and no hand could do more than pluck a few blossoms here and there. In August the whole land waves with leaves and flowers from Maine to Oregon. Then winter comes, invading the vineyards, and harvest fields. Always the north wind leads the armies of destruction. Fierce gales flail the boughs of maple and whip the branches, and the leaves fall in millions. When December comes the forests are bare save where, here and there, the oak leaves adhere to their boughs, like fragile bronze. Now and then a botanist, chilled by the snow, refreshes his memory by looking at the leaves he pressed and the flowers he placed between the pages of his notebook, but it is a far cry from a pressed violet and rose to June bloom and universal summer. These slender reminiscences of Luke's Master represent a few pressed flowers plucked in the garden of his memory. The hand of Luke was made for one golden bough and not for all beautiful forests. In trying to interpret that myriad-minded Master and His efflorescent genius, we must pass from this handful of incidents, this score of parables, to the rich gardens where these flowers were plucked and to the veins of silver and of gold from which this treasure was taken by loving hands. The artist may paint a few canvases, but no painter will ever be a historian of the full summer. The limitations of the human intellect make it certain that the life of Christ will never be written.

Why, then, did Luke and John pass by ninety-nine incidents, and record this particular one?

Man's first duty is to discover himself, who he is, where he came from, what he is here for and whither he is going. But, there is a larger task and a higher knowledge. "Let not the wise man glory in his wisdom, nor the strong man in his strength, nor the rich man in his gold, but let him glory in this, that he understandeth and knoweth God." That which storms can never reveal, that which earthquakes can never proclaim, must be found out by the soul. Every man paints his own portrait of God, but the heart and not the intellect is the artist that limns the canvas. The supreme question is, "How does the Unseen Being feel toward His children, in the hour of their sorrow, suffering, or moral disaster?" In the belief that what Jesus was during three years in Palestine, the all-helpful God is in all ages and lands, the biographers of Jesus selected out of thousands of incidents those episodes that would portray the heart of God, the gentleness of His strength, the mercy of His justice and the tenderness of His verdict upon the career of His children. They passed by the omniscience of God, the wisdom of Jesus, His regency over physical nature, and taking men at the point where the heart is broken and the steps have wandered, they set forth the way that Jesus bore Himself toward the poor pilgrims, lying like bleeding vines torn from the wall, like the snowdrops and anemone, trampled into the ground, by the feet of the multitude.

It is not an accident, therefore, that all four of the biographers of Jesus have told in detail the story of the feast in the home of Simon. Luke alone remembers the parable of the Prodigal Son; Matthew recalls the very words of the Sermon on the Mount; Mark remembers the last charge given the disciples on Olivet, before the Master faded from their sight; John loves to linger over that meeting in the upper room, when the world-untroubled heart released all troubled ones from trouble. But all of the evangelists recall every detail of this exquisite incident that took place at the banquet in the house of that rich man of Bethany.

The host, one may justifiably conjecture, was the leading merchant of his time. His caravans were ever on the road between Jerusalem and the cities of Egypt on the south, and the cities that clustered around Damascus upon the north. Simon dealt in wheat, and wool, and silk, in oil and wine, in spices from Arabia, and gold from Africa, and diamonds from India, and daily he increased in treasure. Tiring of the city, with its din and tumult, he built a rich man's house in the beautiful suburb of Bethany, and there he entertained his guests. From time to time every great city welcomes home the returning hero, the ruler or prince, who represents other lands. Little by little that first citizen of the Hebrew capital, Simon, came to be looked upon as the man who would do the honours for his fellow-men. In those days Jesus was the popular hero. Multitudes pressed and thronged to hear Him speak. The sheer beauty of His words cast a spell upon the multitude. He wove silken threads of truth, and bound men as captives to His chariot. In Him, the poor found a friend. To Him, came the downtrodden, knowing that He would become a voice for their wrongs. The people gave Him their hearts, and thousands would have died for their Teacher. And when, at the end of an excited day, tired inside and tired out, Jesus withdrew to Bethany, this rich man, Simon, with his servants, came out to meet and greet the Master, and took Him, as it were by force, and soon servants spread the feast.

When the news ran around, that the great Teacher was at the rich man's house, merchants closed their stores, farmers left the ploughs in the field, women and children hurried to join the multitudes that filled Simon's house, and crowded his gardens, and overflowed into the street. Great is the power of the soldier! Wonderful the influence of the victor in battles upon land or sea! Most wonderful the power of the statesman, who receives triumphal processions, after some victory over oppression! But more wonderful still the majesty of goodness, the might of love, the regency of a radiant and luminous soul, like Jesus, who, all His life long went up and down the world doing good unto His fellows.

The beauty of this incident and its rich meanings can only be understood through contrasts. Our houses have doors against the chill and rigour of the winter. That house of Simon's was open and built for sunshine and the free movement of the currents of air. To our feasts come only invited guests; ancient feasts were public functions, and the proof that the host was poor was that he limited his invitations, and the proof that Simon was rich was that he had abundance and to spare for all who crossed the threshold of his house. In that far-off era, also, tables were unknown. Guests reclined upon couches, and hours were spent in consuming an unending series of courses of rich foods. When the crowd was densest and there was scarcely room to move, and guests pushed and thronged one against another, a girl who was scarcely more than a child, a girl with a lovely, flower-face, but with robe of sackcloth, suddenly dropped upon her knees and put her arms above the feet of Jesus and bowed her head and burst into a flood of tears. A great silence fell upon the guests. Among those guests were men, perchance, who had reason to know that lovely girl. Perhaps one of them had broken down all the hedges that protect the sweet flowers of the heart in the garden of the soul.

Sometimes the garden gate is left open by the gardener in a thoughtless mood. Then enter the swine, and with tusk and snout root up the soil and grass and crush the snowdrop and the anemone and pull down the fragrant vines that creep over windows and walls. Soon the foul beasts finding the bubbling spring, wallow in the pure water and turn it into mire. They find a garden, they leave bleeding vines and bruised flowers. This girl had suffered much at the hands of evil men, who had placed in her hand the cup of flame, and with lying pledges lured her from the paths of peace into tropic jungles, where blooms the scarlet upas flowers, flowers growing in fetid jungles, where death and putrefaction have their secret lair. But now at last all illusions have dissolved, the mirage has faded, the wreaths on the forehead of passion have withered, the lights have burned low in the socket, the night has fallen, the wind is chill, the storm clouds thicken, the windows begin to rattle, the wind sobs and sighs in the chimney. Voices of remorse threaten, and partly in a mood of fear and partly in shame, but most of all through sorrow and repentance, in a great, wild orgasm of confession, this sweet girl comes to herself! Her tears fall like rain upon the Master's feet.

Oh, these blessed tears! Not the dewdrop is so pure! This child feared lest her tears scald His person, and loosing her hair she made a veil behind which she could hide her face, and with the long tresses she wiped His feet, and took that sweet ointment, very precious, used only for great occasions, and broke the treasure-box for the Master. Sometimes men sweep a half-acre of red roses into one little vial, filled with their precious attar; and in those far-off days, experts distilled certain precious perfumes, and breaking not only the outer alabaster box, but that secret box of love, she poured out all the wealth of her soul upon the Master.

Be it remembered that in that era the debtor, in asking mercy from his creditor, bowed at the feet of his benefactor; that the slave and disciple knelt at the foot of the master's couch and in embracing the feet surrendered the very life in devotion to the lord of the life. And in fulfillment of one of the customs understood by all those guests, this woman surrendered herself and by the symbolic act made herself for evermore the slave to flawless purity and perfect justice and the divine love of the Master. It is only when we study the scenes and the unfolding chapters in the life of this young girl that we understand the exquisite beauty of an act that has made immortal the doer. We know not her name, we cannot measure the wealth of her love; the act without represented the sentiment of the soul within, but unconsciously she has built a monument more enduring than marble or bronze. Her life opened with a tender pastoral scene that we can reproduce even as an expert can replace the amethyst torn from its matrix and original setting. One night her father returned from the city to his home in the country. His daughter, wearing a simple white dress, with one flower at her throat, met him at the garden gate and clasped both hands about his arm. She took him through the flower beds, not knowing that she herself was the sweetest flower that had bloomed under that sun. What anemones midst the grass! What violets hidden under the leaves! There also were orange blossoms and on the same boughs the ripened fruit. And there with her own hands she had fastened the honeysuckle vine above the door and made the entrance to the house to be drenched with fragrance. She had spread the simple meal in a little summer-house, and upon the white cloth she had placed the cold water from the spring. Then she lifted the leaves and showed him the strawberries she had just plucked and the thick cream all waiting, and the wheaten loaf, and trying to make him forget the toil of the day she drew him to his chair and put one arm around his shoulder and laid her face against his bronzed cheek and whispered, "Oh, father, I am so happy!" And crushing the sweet child to his breast the proud father forgot his tire and felt himself to be a king, and for one brief moment forgot his loneliness for her mother, so long since passed away. Wearing the child like a rose upon his heart, he bore himself like a king and walked the earth, a monarch among those who served.

Then came dark days. A serpent entered that garden. Mephistopheles conspired against young Marguerite. With fiendish skill he sought to break down the hedge, and destroy the buttresses that protect virtue. Then came a tragedy, oh, how black! It was the season for the games and sports, and races of an age all too vulgar. All streets were thronged, and all race-tracks. The air was filled with the dust of chariots, and runners and horsemen. Vendors of their wares lifted up shrill voices, and cried aloud. And moving slowly through the scene went the Master and Lord of life. At last the Carpenter stayed His steps before a house of pleasure. Around one banqueting table sat a company of wild and reckless young men and women. And lo! The central figure, toward whose face all these half-drunken young men leaned, and to whom they stretched out the ripened grapes, the fresh figs, the fragrant sweetmeats, stands—that of the young girl of the garden, but with face, oh, how changed! And even as Jesus stays His steps beside that table she rises in her place, to drink a health, and drunken boys empty beakers into her overflowing glass, and the purple flood runs down and stains the cloth. Stopping before that table Jesus looked straight into the girl's eyes. Oh, those all-seeing eyes of Jesus! Eyes that knew all, understood all, and pitied all! No swords were in those eyes. No sparks of fire leaped forth. No arm was lifted to smite, but Jesus stood there, a great, dear presence, with rebuke of love and pain and disappointment! The girl stood transfixed, her lips parted, in wonder she stretched out that little, right hand, holding that enpurpled cup as if to ask, "Who art thou?" Astounded, the revelers rise slowly to their feet. In astonishment they gaze first at the queen of the feast, and then at the strange Teacher, while they ask what these things may mean. Suddenly, she drops the goblet that, falling, breaks upon the table. She lifts her hands and tears away the scarlet flowers twisted in her hair. She strips the pearls from her throat and flings them upon the stones beneath. Still looking into the Master's eyes, she pulls off the rings and jeweled bracelets, and when the Master turns and covers His face with His hand because the pain of it was more than He could bear, she breathes forth one sobbing moan like a young and wounded thing, and sinks unconscious in the chair, as the shadows and dark night close around and veil the scene!

And now, we behold another scene. Once more that young girl is back in her father's garden. The silent looks of that great Teacher had dissolved all the illusions of pleasure and sin. What had seemed ambrosia became the apples of Sodom, filled with ashes and soot. What once was the wine of Bacchus and the nectar of Venus, became as the droppings of asps and the poison of serpents. Those scarlet flowers that her lover had twisted into a wreath became like coals of fire, blistering her forehead. In her long pursuit of the god of pleasure, suddenly, that whom she had pursued turned, and instead of the face of some ideal youth she found she had embraced a toothless hag, and she shrieked aloud. In her black despair, she returned to the home, knowing she would find it empty because her sin had slain her father, and lo, the garden of her youth had come up to weeds, as toads and lizards ran across the garden walks. Fallen the vines from the bare windows! Gone all the sweet flowers! Rain had come through the roof. Mould was upon the walls. In an abandon of grief, she flung her face upon the garden grass and with dry sobs, her little fingers clutched the earth, while she called on death. Soon she plucked away each soft garment and in an old closet found sackcloth and black, and she hid herself until the night fell. Then, standing in the shadows, she stood in the outskirts of the multitude, and listened to that strange Teacher, and once she drew nearer, and despite her veil found that the Master had recognised her. Suddenly, He lifted His hand and, looking straight over the heads of other hearers to that place where she stood, He sent across the space one word for her heart alone: " I am come to seek and save that which is lost." Some inner voice whispered: " He speaks to you."

No mariner on a dark and stormy night, upon a

dangerous coast ever longed for the lighthouse that should lead into the harbour as that young girl had longed for the light, and now it had flamed forth. At last, the light had come! Shaken with joy, while hope and fear wrestled in her heart, she turned and fled back to that deserted garden, but all night long, and all the next day the bells of hope kept ringing, and in her dreams she found herself again tossed in the dark upon the yeasty sea, and ever across the flood came that sweet and mellow bell, "I am come to seek and save that which is lost," and when she wakened it was as if a night of storm, with hissing winds and trembling earth, and sheeted flames and forked lightning had all passed, and left the flowers safe, and the garden sweet, and lo, the birds were singing again in the branches as a great peace stole into her heart.

When the night fell, with transports of joy, she heard that the Master was at the house of the rich merchant, Simon, and entering with the great throng, and concealing her face behind her robe, she suddenly finds herself beside His couch. Love always finds a way. The heart needs no guide and no protector. One look into His face told her heart that she had not deceived herself. What wonder words were those she heard? What did this mean that the Master should have asked Simon about the two creditors, and now, when the man who owed a vast debt, and the man whose debt was a trifle alike could pay nothing, that the creditor freely forgave them both? And what did this silence mean that fell upon the other guests at the question as to which debtor loved the benefactor most? And then came the answer, "I suppose that he loved most to whom most was forgiven." And in that moment she bowed her head and in a transport of joy she wept aloud as she heard the words "Thy sins are forgiven thee. Go in peace." Wheresoever this story shall be told, it shall be a monument to her. Since that far-off time centuries have come and gone, but the story comes like a strain of sweet music sounding down the long aisles of time, and the fragrance of that box of ointment lingers and now perfumes all literature and lends sweetness to the wide-lying world.

The lessons of this exquisite scene in the life of the Redeemer, are like flowers waiting to be plucked in God's rich garden. How plain it is that there are unrevealed treasures hidden under all the wreck of sin and shame. History tells us that the fire that followed the earthquake in Athens, revealed, when the ashes were carried away, unsuspected veins of silver. But what hidden gold in every heart? In God's sight all men go forward, big with latent treasures. It is as if the farmer valued the field for its vegetables and grain, because his is a surface view. It is as if Simon had looked upon this sinning woman's life as upon a garden filled with weeds, thorns and thistles, while the Lord of the garden, with all-seeing eye, pierced through the crust and saw beneath the soil with its mire-hidden veins of gold and crystals waiting to be cut into diamonds—as if all flashing rubies and sapphires were waiting to be uncovered.

Nor must we forget that other lesson, the judgment of perfect goodness upon the sins of the human heart, and the mercy of God's justice in whispering His verdict upon the deeds of the soul. Too often we have closed this revelation of the heart of God to open the Bible to statements about the wrath of an avenging law-giver. Philosophers have invoked the support of isolated texts, "Our God is a consuming fire," "The fear of the Lord is the beginning of wisdom," and so forth, forgetting that Jesus bore Himself in such a way as to reveal how God feels toward all erring ones who have left the paths of truth and virtue. As men go toward genius and greatness and the uttermost of holiness, they go toward gentleness in judgment. The Master and Lord of life, with His stainless perfection, was very pitiful. Sinful men would have fain stoned this girl. Perfect love, with instant pity, forgave her. Nor would He even permit her to tell her story. "Daughter"—ah, what a word was that! How long had she waited for someone to say the word that used often to fall from the lips of her revered father, long since dead. And now, that home word, "Daughter," that bosom pressure word, "My child," had fallen from the lips of the greatest among the holy, and the purest among the great. It was like water to a dying wanderer, perishing of thirst in the desert. It was like music falling from the battlements of Heaven. What wonder words were these that fell upon her bleeding and broken heart; "Thy sins are forgiven thee, go in peace." In that moment, the flare of lightning passed away, the black cloud on the horizon dissolved, the last echo of the midnight storm and tornado ceased to exist, the sun shone forth and in her vision she saw her father and mother coming across the grass in the souls' summerland, to take her into their arms and whisper welcome and lead her up unto the throne of mercy, not marble, the throne of love, and not a law. And when the Master spoke the word "Forgiven" every wound was healed, as she entered her Paradise, and her hot desert became an Eden garden.

VI

SOME WHO ARE OFFENDED

"And they were offended at him."—MARK vi: 3.

IN that far-off era, when certain leaders were offended by Jesus, there were many forms of pride and shame. Most beautiful were some of their cities, and there must have been a Theban pride, a Roman pride, and an Ephesian pride. Revolting, too, the ugliness and squalor of many regions, and men must have been ashamed of the slave and the gladiator, of rags and crusts, of the gibbet and the scourge and the dungeon. And some men there were who listened to the teachings of Jesus, and were offended by His plain speech. The rulers of the city were men of vast property, and old family memories, while Jesus was a peasant —and they were offended by Him. The scribes were men of culture and training, and Jesus was an untaught carpenter, and these were offended. The chief priests were at the head of the Established Church, with its splendid temple, its historic ritual, and gorgeous vestments and clouds of incense, while Jesus was a carpenter, teaching the people up on the hillside, and these men, also, were offended by Him.

The region of Galilee held many Grecian towns and illustrated Grecian art, Grecian culture and literature, and these Greeks were offended with Jesus. At last public sentiment organised itself, and a mob went forth with stones to wreak its fury on the carpenter's son and brought Him to His death. And the story of His ignominy and shame shocked the proud Roman soldier, and the imperious merchant from Greece. The Jew, because he was a Jew, was a thorn rankling in the side of the nations of that era. And when this Nazarene teacher outlined a universal religion, a world-wide sway and a golden age, when His teachings should be supreme, men were offended. Little by little these feelings of resentment gathered depth, power and momentum. Piling up like waters behind the dam, at last the floods of indignation swept away all barriers, and the Galilæan teacher was overwhelmed with death, through earth's most piteous tragedy. So odious was the Cross that the very manner of His dying became an offense, and the multitudes melted away. Their enthusiasm concerning Him disappeared like dew on the grass. His cause was a lost cause, and His star sunk in a disaster that seemed irretrievable and forever.

Lo, today, all has changed! Time has lent rich associations to a name that once was poor and scant. Looking backward, we behold Jesus through an atmosphere roseate and golden, through glorious associations! History has become a kind of long cathedral aisle, crowded with splendid tablets and memorials of the Master. Slowly all that is most glorious in art, architecture and philanthropy has united to lend beauty to this sublime

Name. For thoughtful men, shame toward Jesus has become unthinkable. Shame is a downward-looking quality. Men are ashamed toward drunkenness and gluttony, toward rags and vice and crime, toward the poor-house and the jail. Pride is an upward-looking quality; men are proud toward the cathedral, and the palace and the library, toward eminence, influence and immortal fame. In contrast with other great names, Jesus has become the central figure in history. Offense now seems impossible. How glorious His teachings! How winsome and alluring His gentle life! Innumerable reforms have sprung from His kindness toward children, outcasts and the broken-hearted poor.

No hand can be found willing to tarnish Christ's portrait. Today not a tongue is foul enough to speak evil of His character and career. His music seems world music, that pierces all hearts with its sweetness. His influence has become a contagion—a contagion of happiness and beauty and help. Whatsoever makes for greatness stirs longing and delight. Under that influence, as travellers, we make long pilgrimages to the little house where the great poet was born, to the room where the dramatist penned his greatest page. We uncover under the sublime dome that an architect's hand hath lifted. Collectors pay fortunes vying with one another for the possession of the sword of some soldier, a missal by some old master, a manuscript by some great author. From these relics of genius the possessor borrows a reflected light and glory. But he who associates his name with the name of

Jesus stands in a blaze of effulgent light, light intellectual, light pure and spiritual; a light and beauty that can never wane. And these affiliations of Christianity, and the achievements of Jesus are calculated to evoke only pride and admiration in devoted and lofty souls.

But despite all the associations of history, let us confess that today some are offended, and have gone away from Christ and His Church. They concede the beauty of Christ's character, they are conscious of His increasing world influence, they are in sympathy with the objects for which His followers are toiling, but they deny the necessity of any open alliance with His cause. It is said by many that those within the Church are no better than those without it. The critic exclaims, "I would put my life as an outsider against that man's life as an insider; my honesty against his honesty; my business career against his business career." But we concede at the outset that now and then a man outside of the Church, by virtue of his birth-gifts, is equal to or even superior to some men's achievements, even with all the help of the Church —on the inside. But this argues nothing save the superiority of the native gifts of the one man who received much, and was made self-sufficing by God and His fathers while the other man received little, and needs every possible form of help.

We confess that Abraham Lincoln, never having been in college, can write better English than Edward Everett, president of Harvard University. Does that justify you in railing at colleges, and refusing assistance to them? John Bunyan wrote the second book in English literature. Ought we therefore to refuse support to Oxford and Cambridge? Some self-made men there are of gifts so unique that they can succeed without any external helps and appliances, but perhaps they would have achieved more signal success with them. The Church is a means to an end, and does not exist for its own sake. The Church is a college in morals, a university of right living, a culture-room where the laws of life are studied and practised. It is a school to which men are admitted because they are ignorant, and want to become wise, who are weak and want to become strong, who are bad and want to become good. A church is like the steps leading into a beautiful mansion, but you do not sit down on the steps, you do not set up a tent on the steps, you do not live on the steps—the steps lift you to the level of the warm room, the blazing winter's fire, the bower of home that receives you out of the driving rain or pelting snow. All the ordinances of the Church are steps that lead to the house of character, adorned with all those rich treasures, named truth, gentleness, meekness and justice and sympathy. The Church is a hostelry in which man stops for a night on his journey home. The end of the Church is character, likeness to Christ, automatic goodness and solid weight of character.

Some men of high ideals are offended by the mistakes and sins of those within the Church, just as once men were offended at Peter's denial, and Judas' treason, and John's cowardice, and Saul's cruelty. Now, we hold no brief to defend every man who has joined the Church. We only ask whether, in fair play, it is in order to rail at an institution because of the blunders of some identified therewith? Of course, there are men in churches who stumble and fall prostrate. Of course, also, there are bankers and cashiers who have stumbled, and a hundred and fifty of them, possibly, last year, made their way to Mexico or Africa. There are jurists who are tempted and fall; there are more than a hundred lawyers who are now living at state expense in Sing Sing. There are merchants who crowd their shelves with empty pasteboard boxes, and then have a fire. Do you feel it is necessary to withdraw from business because these dishonest men are in it? Suppose the youth should refuse marriage and the obligations of husband and father because some men and women quarrel in the home?

There are orchards that are worthless through neglect. In New England stands an orchard that at one time was one tangle of thickets. For years no pruner's knife had been lifted upon the bough. The splendid trees had been permitted to run to branch, until the woody fibre drank up all the substance and left nothing for the fruit. The boughs were one teeming, putrescent mass of caterpillars' nests; rabbits had gnawed at the bark, and moles had cut the roots, and every crack and seam was filled with parasites that sapped away the trees' life. Neglect had ruined the noble orchard. Cruel enemies had stripped it of its power. The sun shone only upon small, gnarled, bitter fruit, that might have been rich as the apples of Paradise.

Outside, in the lane, however, grew one young apple tree. From its smooth boughs schoolboys shook a little fruit. But did that little tree in the lane, that happened to be well-born and surrounded with sunshine, prove that orchards are a failure? It was not the orchard that failed—it was a lazy husbandman failed, a careless, drunken farmer failed, a man failed, but not the orchard principle. And the Church is a kind of vineyard and orchard, established by the Divine Husbandman, as a method of soul culture. Character is a fruit that is ripened by daily toil and unremitting care. Industry must lift the spade, prudence must guard against unseen enemies, prayer must call down rain and dew from heaven; the soul must have the summer atmosphere. These rich fruits do not come by chance. Character is an achievement, and the Church is an orchard Eden, for those who commune with God, under the boughs of the trees.

Others there are who have accepted the philosophy of Rousseau. They wish to cast the reins loose upon the neck of passion, and permit their appetites to carry them whithersoever they will. "I want to be free, to lead my own life in my own way." They say, the real life is the untrammelled life—the bird life, the wild horse life, that never takes on the yoke, or feels the rein, or endures the scourge. They talk about the return to Nature, and point to the Bohemian career. But stop and reflect. Consider that no man ever added to his obligations to gravity by acknowledging gravity, or escaped the law of gravity by refusing obedience thereto. Natural laws do not ask whether or not we give allegiance to them. Duty is something that must be done. No man increases his obligations by joining a church, and no man lessens his obligations by refusing that allegiance. We owe obedience to the laws of God, not because we are church members, but because we are men. All who are born into a cradle and die into a grave are in God's great world, under the sway of His laws, open to His rewards incident to obedience, and subject to the penalties of disobedience and sin. Here is a boy who enters the bank. When his employer finds his column of figures full of mistakes, the boy becomes angry, saying: "I never went to school and promised to obey the laws of the multiplication table. I am an outsider. I don't propose to lose my liberty by promising to keep the laws of mathematics."

Here is some lover who sends a letter to one who scorns the words that are misspelled, and laughs at the writer's poor rhetoric. But the youth answers: "I refuse to join the school. I never stood up in the class-room and promised to obey the laws of spelling and orderly thinking." And here is the young glutton, or drunkard, or disciple of pleasure, saying, when disease racks him, and pains overtake him: "I never promised to obey the laws of temperance, and prudence, and of God." Well, Nature is a very severe teacher, and a stern judge. Whether you promise to obey the laws of God or not, Nature will deal out her judgments impartially. You escape no law by refusing obedience; you escape no duty by remaining without the Church; you cannot escape from God's world until you can lift yourself out of the all-encompassing air. There is no land to which you can flee, that you may have license to be lawless. Freedom comes through obedience to law. Happiness follows the surrender of the will unto God. The path of duty is the path to glory without and to peace within. Remember that every man without the Church is under every obligation of the man within the Church; for duty is not binding upon us as churchmen; duty is binding upon us because we are in God's world, supported by His bounty, and under the obligations incident to His mercy and His love.

Some there are who are offended by Christ's words, "He that saveth his life shall lose it; he who loveth father or mother more than Me is not worthy of Me." They interpret these words to mean asceticism, the denial of pleasure, and the refusal of every cup of honied delight. To be a Christian for them is to wear sackcloth, enter a lifelong retreat; to refuse the ear music, and the eye beauty; to deny the heart friendship; to turn one's face toward a desert of waste and desolation and monotony. They think of the proverb that Jesus was often seen to weep, but never known to laugh—a grievous misstatement and perversion of facts. How could Jesus have been other than the happiest of men? What joy pervades a great Teacher's heart? What delight comes to him who, entering the garret, can, through his gold become bread to the hungry, and warmth to the naked, and medicine to the sick? When the peasants delivered by Garibaldi fell upon their knees and kissed his hands, do you think their emancipator felt no happiness? Jesus passed through the world like a prince, scattering treasure on every hand. He healed the sick, delivered the prisoners, comforted the hopeless, blessed the children, lifted up the fallen, gave life to the dying. And oh, what happiness came into His heart, with all the might of a rushing storm, with the richness of the summer's wind! Jesus knew the joy of living, the passion of happiness, the rage of life. For us, happiness is a little rivulet, covering the feet; for Jesus, joy was a river deep enough to swim in, an ocean in whose depths He bathed His soul. And for the children of God all good things exist—all the sweetness of music, the beauty of art, the grandeur of architecture, the majesty of the summers and the sanctity of the winters; all the treasures of literature and art and friendship; all the riches of the waters under the earth; all these are yours because "ye are Christ's and Christ is God's."

Of course the lower pleasures are not yours, but there are pleasures and pleasures. Tomorrow you may meet a tramp on the Bowery, all rags, and blear-eyed, a mass of dirt and disease. And suppose you offer him a home, plead with him for temperance, and offer him work in the country, and ask him to swear fidelity to his mother's memory and his father's God? At which the wreck turns his bleared eyes and his purple, mildewed lips toward some low saloon, and says, "No, I cannot give up these pleasures. You ask me to sacrifice too much. Let me have these delights a little longer." The pleasures! The pleasure of an outraged digestion! The pleasures of inflamed nerves! The pleasures of picking crusts out of an ash-barrel and the delights of bilge water! The happiness incident to leading a swine's life! But, young man, this is epic of your own career. You stand one or two steps higher, to be sure; yet, looking toward covetousness, and yielding to avarice, and the desire for rude position, you seek places and are not willing to give up these low pleasures for the pleasure of an approving conscience, and the smile of a loving Father, and the feeling that you have obeyed the great convictions of the soul, and have entered upon the task of the patriot and scholar, and the patrician Christian. The Good is an enemy of the Better, and the Better is an enemy of the Best.

Fling yourself into the Christian life with abandon, and you will find the highest happiness, happiness that is all persuasive, a sacred peace, a tranquility that pervades the whole being, a companionship that makes loneliness impossible. The youth who enters upon the Christian life finds unanticipated rewards. He is like a man who buys a field for wheat, but, digging, finds coal, and mining for coal, strikes iron, and, surprised as he digs for iron, discovers silver, and below that, suddenly gold appears! From the viewpoint of the mining engineer, such strata are impossible, but as an illustration of the soul's unsuspected discoveries and treasures, the illustration is not only permissible, but represents a great solid fact. Therefore, I call you to the Christian life. I call you to a surrender of the will, to the supreme allegiance of conscience, to the dedication of mind and heart to the Master and Saviour of the World. Enter this school, and begin the highest form of culture. Plant your faculties like roots that shall grow unto goodly vines. Sow your thoughts and deeds like seeds, and reap therefrom white harvests. Build your character like a cathedral and decorate it with the faces of ideals and angels and seraphs. Root your life in occupation and industry, in the earth beneath, but remember that the flowers acquire their fragrance and beauty from the heavens above.

VII

THE BEAUTY OF THE CHRISTIAN LIFE

"Finally, brethren, whatsoever things are true, whatsoever things are honest, whatsoever things are just, whatsoever things are pure, whatsoever things are lovely, whatsoever things are of good report; if there be any virtue, and if there be any praise, think on these things."—PHIL. iv: 8.

ABRAHAM LINCOLN once said that he was going to join a church just as soon as he found one that believed in love to God and love to man. Once, during three wonderful years there was this ideal church upon our earth, all ready for some Lincoln to join. Then everybody knew precisely what it was to be a Christian. A Christian was one who followed Christ, who prayed to the heavenly Father, and who could sincerely say, "I believe in the Beatitudes, I believe in forgiving my enemies, I believe in giving a cup of cold water to the poor and the weak, I believe in being kind and gentle, and in helping the poor."

At that time, Jesus was the only Christian in the world, but He made the Christian life so alluring that His disciples went toward it as naturally as the birds go toward a bower of roses. Men could no more misunderstand it than they could misunderstand a purple cluster or a sheaf of wheat. The very children beholding Jesus, felt they could be His disciples, just as the noblest saints came to feel that they could never overtake Christ's divine beauty. The whole emphasis of Jesus was upon goodness and character. He placed no emphasis upon books, for He never wrote one; nor upon a church, for He never organised one; nor upon a government, creed or catechism, for He passed by all of them.

Jesus was not a hero of the sword, nor a hero of gold, nor a hero of the forum. He was the hero of a life, beautiful and alluring. Asked what it was to be a Christian, the disciples pointed to Jesus. Asked to define patriotism, the historian answers "Washington." Asked to define statesmanship, the scholar answers "Daniel Webster." Asked to define intellect, the philosopher answers "Plato, and Aristotle." Asked to define the Christian, we answer "Jesus Christ." That name binds together all possible excellencies, just as the string binds together a thousand golden heads of wheat.

For thoughtful men, the Christian life seems the only natural and normal life. Rousseau led a movement back to Nature. The Frenchman's influence was at once good and bad. The movement away from artificiality was wholesome and healthy, but it was a bad thing to move from ripe back to the raw, from the oak back to the acorn, from the house back to the cave in which a savage man dwelt, from the restraints of wise laws back to the unbridled passions of forest children. What France needed was a movement not back toward the beginnings of things, but forward toward full

Nature. What is Nature? Is Nature the scrub oak? Is not Nature the acorn carried forward to an acre-covering oak? What is the strawberry? Is that tiny, sour berry, growing on the edge of an Arctic snowdrift, a strawberry? Or is Nature the strawberry carried up to its best estate in the largest and sweetest berry that grows in England?

The babe begins at nothing and slowly goes toward full manhood. The child begins a mere handful of seeds, a bough of unblossomed buds, and gradually unfolds. Slowly the intellect grows toward the wisdom of a sage. Slowly, the scholar's memory unfolds into universal knowledge. No child of today starts with original arithmetic, nor original geography, nor original science, nor original tools, nor original character. Under the infiuence of God's Spirit goodness is achieved.

But man learns by example. Once the pupil beholds the work of the artist-master, he understands. It is the parent who is the best pattern, counsellor and guide for the child. Not otherwise our race needed a typical man, as an exemplar, and Jesus entered the scene as the first natural and normal man. Was it not Charles Lamb who said that Jesus was "the world's first gentleman"? Plainly the divine Carpenter standardised character and gave something by which to measure progress. His whole emphasis was upon ethics. No young inventor can understand himself until he studies Watt, Kelvin or Edison. No young poet can ever understand his possibilities until he studies Shakespeare, just as no artist can understand the beautiful and his own capacity to interpret loveliness until he has lingered long before some Rembrandt. And neither John nor Paul could ever have understood their own latent capacity for heroism and martyrdom, but for the example of Jesus. What Jesus was, every man must try to be. But no man understood that possible goal until Jesus had lived, and taught and died. He was the earth's first natural and normal man, telling the race what God and His divine resources can accomplish upon each human soul.

Consider the beauty of the Christian life as illustrated by Jesus. It is inevitable that the natural and normal life shall blossom into the life that is beautiful. No living thing, from violet and arbutus to oak and pine, can fulfill the law of its being without at last coming into loveliness. At first, the bulb is ugly, but if it obey the secret voice, it will flower into the tulip's brilliancy. At first the sweetbriar is covered with thorns, but if it work steadily along its own line, it will suddenly flame up in crimson and white. Whoever obeys the law of his work will find that beauty is his crown. Obey the law of speech and you will have eloquence. Obey the laws of form and colour and young Giotto will have a masterpiece. Obey the laws of writing and you have literature. Obey the law of morals, and you have adorned and made beautiful the doctrine of God your Saviour. And once a true disciple stands forth fully revealed, and like Christ, you have the best thing our earth has to offer—a golden sheaf waving its beauty, back into the God of summer.

The Christian life wears bright colours, where

any other life whatsoever wears black. The Christian life holds all sweet music, where any other life whatsoever holds a funeral dirge. The Christian life holds all lilies and roses, all flowers and fruits, while other lives are Sahara sand or Arctic ice. Men have been infidel to the deeds of Joshua, infidel toward Inquisitions, infidel toward creed, and catechisms. Men have been infidel toward bigotry and intolerance, but no man ever lived who was infidel to the true Christian life. What a string of flowers and fruits Paul assembled in describing the beauty of the Christian! The child plucks the raspberries, black or red, and strings them on a blade of grass, and the berries, overfull of juices, break, and the purple flood runs down, and Paul's words drip with the nectar and wine of loveliness.

Call the roll of these beautiful traits—" Whatsoever things are true." Think you any man ever can be infidel to the truths of earth and sun, as stated by Newton? How can any noble scholar be infidel toward Phocion, Socrates, or Lincoln? Did any youth ever withhold admiration from the splendid deed of Jeanie Deans? Is there any heart so base that it can withhold tears in the moment when Jean Valjean speaks truth to his own hurt and changes not? Overwhelmed with the loveliness of Truth, all men bow down to kiss the hem of her garment.

" Whatsoever things are pure "—was any man ever infidel to purity? To the whiteness of the cloud? The clarity of the dewdrop? The loveliness of the rainbow? Is any man vile enough to be infidel to the innocence of the babe? the delicacy of the maiden? the purity of a noble woman? to the spotlessness of an unblemished scholar, or statesman?

"Whatsoever things are lovely and of good report"—was any man ever infidel toward name and reputation? The Christian life "is love," and all the world loves a lover. No youth was ever infidel to the love that breathes and pulsates like flame through the *Sonnets from the Portuguese* of Elizabeth Barrett Browning. A person is educated in love in proportion to his appreciation of these supreme visions, just as the poet is educated in proportion as he knows Dante or Milton. Was any man ever infidel to "joy" in a world where all are in a scramble to overtake happiness through music, the drama, or social pleasures? Was any man ever infidel to the peace manifest in the face of an old man who has come victorious out of all the thunder of life's battle? Was any ever infidel toward long-suffering as illustrated in the patience of the brave soldier, the heroic father, the self-sacrificing mother or wife? Earth holds no such flowers as these that bloom in the garden of the Christian life. Kings own no such strings of jewels as these gems called the fruits of the spirit, that glow and sparkle like the stars, having undying luster. Beholding Christ and the beauty of His life, we can only exclaim,—"How great is His goodness and how great is His beauty!"

Consider that the Christian life is the life of growth. We are in the world to grow, and grow, and *still* grow. Jesus comes to fill the soul with noble discontent. Nothing is stationary and unchanging after His spirit is received. Each victory is only a place where the disciple sets up his tent for the night, to march forward to new achievements on the morrow. Men do not join themselves to Christ's glorious company because they are perfect, but because they wish to be perfect. Strange that men should say, "I am not good enough to join a church, and as soon as I feel that I am, I will enter this beautiful company." Does a youth enter college because he knows all about science and literature? Does he not make application to the college just because he is ignorant of science and literature? Does the boy enter the school of fine arts because he can paint, or that he may learn to paint? We found institutions of law and medicine to teach men the principles of law or to teach the hand skill in surgery. Peter and John did not wait until they were perfect to join Christ's disciple band. They were ignorant, and Jesus asked them to follow Him that they might become wise. They were raw, selfish and crude, and Jesus asked them to follow Him that He might, by daily companionship and unceasing guidance, make them large and mature, struck through and through with sweetness and light.

The first processes of carpentry are easy, but not the higher carving. The stone-cutter's task is easy at the beginning, but the final stage of shaping the statue at the head is very difficult. There is always room at the top, because the topmost duties are artistic and delicate and most complex, and few climb thereto. The early stages of the Christian life, when the man forswears gluttony, vulgarity, and so forth, are simple. Lingering on the outskirts of the crowd, rude John Bunyan said, as he listened to a wonderful teacher, "Now I must not drink any more, I must not fish on Sundays, I must not swear—not out loud,"—and so John Bunyan begins. The beginning was like digging the cellar for a new mansion—it was very easy work. But each new tier of stone for the first story and the second grows more difficult, and when, finally, the mansion is to be decorated, then the highest gifts of imagination are called for, and those artists named Faith and Hope and Love slowly cover the walls with the faces of angels and seraphs. Surely, that is a task for archangels! That Bunyan, who began with rude foundation work, ends the life task with the delicate artistry of God. It is not easy to be a great singer, or a great painter, or a great architect, or a great poet, but the most difficult thing in the world is to be a great Christian. For everything that is right, and true, and beautiful in nature, art or science, everything in land or sea and sky belongs to God and Christ, and therefore, to the Christian, who must at last stand forth "a citizen of the universe."

If, however, the Christian life is the freest and the happiest of lives, it is also the life that carries forth redemption for others. The difference between the scholars of Athens and the disciple of Jesus is that one carries the cultural note that may be selfish and the other carries the distributive note that diffuses happiness on every side. No philosopher of Athens ever braved the jungles of Africa to be a teacher! No Athenian poet or orator ever dared martyrdom to teach savages the art of eloquence or song. The very essence of Athenian culture was self-love, an ambition to achieve personal development, while the essence of the Christian life is the impulse to serve others, and sow the whole world with happiness and good will.

Christ is abroad upon a mission of recovery, to seek and save the lost. He put His hands about the publican, who farmed out the taxes, and was the best-hated man of his time, and slowly Jesus led him back to loyalty and patriotism. Having the redemptive spirit, Jesus sought out the blind man who had been expelled from the Temple, and with kindness healed his wounded heart. When cruel men pursued that sinning woman, and would have stoned her to death, Jesus made Himself a shield for her protection, a barrier against their cruelty and hate. Only once in a generation is it given to us to witness an illustration of this act of Christ.

Years ago, a young lawyer unable to endure the New England climate, made his way into the West. He was a graduate of college and law school, and a man of splendid gifts. He had not been himself exempt from temptation. It is not necessary to explain how he had met a young girl of seventeen or thereabouts, a mere child, who had been snared by silken threads, tempted and assailed, until little by little all the ledges that protect youth had been broken down. Beautiful was the girl, most beautiful! But all of the sweet flowers of the soul had been torn down, like a vine torn from its doorway! In one great outburst of pity the young lawyer said: "Leave this life. I will take you to an Eastern school for girls. When you have graduated I will make a home for you, and give you my name." It was too astounding to be true, and the girl disbelieved for joy! Soon with the beginning of love came the revelation of unworthiness. One day he took the child away to a distant state, and placed her in a school for young women. For weeks she moved as gently as if her feet were shod with velvet. At last, angered by the questions of a companion who did not understand, the girl flamed out in fiery speech, and horrified all who heard the outburst. Horrified teachers locked her in a closet, and telegraphed for that lawyer. Once, twice, thrice, he began again, but the greater her need the greater his love. Three full years came and went again, and she graduated from the girl's school, and when she returned West, to that mountain state city, she returned with his name. But the struggle had overtaxed his strength, and his old enemy, always lying in wait, tuberculosis, returned to the attack. For seven years she fought for his life, holding him up as death pulled him down the descent.

Kneeling one Sunday afternoon beside that man's bed, I heard a little moan. I saw a woman hanging over a man lying with closed eyes, and with the faintest possible breath. All the lamps of love were aflame. She loved as the tigress loves. She hung over that man as the mother-eagle hangs over her young for protection. She was not one woman—she was a thousand women. Her hands were not strong simply; they were hands that had the strength of archangels. It was not adoration; it was adoration and love carried up to the nth power. Oh, the flame of it upon that woman's face! Once seen, it could never be forgotten. It is a flame seldom kindled. Not one man in a thousand ever heard such love words! She had been forgiven much, and she loved much! Perhaps not many women in a generation love as that woman loved. Love heaved her soul, as the tide heaves the sea! Love pulsated through her face as iron boils and pulsates, with secret heat and light.

The love names she poured upon that dying man's bed held such things as no Dante ever said of Beatrice. The dying lawyer deserved it all. But what that lawyer did for that bruised flower, God, in His redemptive love, is always doing for us. The first sign of a true Christian is this redemptive instinct, this desire to recover others out of the storm, the hail and night, into the Eden of happiness and peace.

O all ye young hearts! Consider well this beautiful and alluring life! Not to a monkish life, not to an artificial life, are you called, but to a free, full-orbed, vitalised, rich, luminous life of complete manhood! Do not spend the richness of your youth upon yourself and then give the embers and ashes of a wasted career to the Master of us all! Considerations of honour suggest generosity toward God. If very early you begin the practice and the study of law, medicine and business, begin even earlier the practice of the Christian life. Remember how short the time is. At best you have all too little time in a world where the years dissolve like snowflakes in a river. Uncertain also the future.

Wise toward your house and store, you insure goods. Be not careless, therefore, about the treasures of the soul. All things else will go, your houses will rot, the tools will rust, riches take wings and even health will at last leave you! As your strength lessens, your offices and honours will go to others who have stronger hands. Death, too, will war against you, and soon you will be solitary, because your own generation will have gone. If your soul is like a great mansion do not be afraid to renovate the rooms. Have you locked up the room where conscience lives? Are there skeletons hidden away in that room over which memory presides? Light the lamp and search out every hidden thing. From time to time the housewife cleanses the garret and cellar and with antiseptics sweetens all things! If women are prudent about things that perish, should you be reckless about things of the soul, that abide forever? Pluck up by the roots the poison plant and deadly nightshade. In these days make the life a garden in which new wondrous plants and flowers shall soon be growing. Remember that your life is not in these things that are seen. It is given unto summer to make all things new in pasture and field! And with what form of transformation? The voice that bids the seeds waken is not the voice of thunder. The stroke that the Angel of Summer lays upon the root is not the stroke of the earthquake. The rain clouds do not thunder forth the coming of Summer. The Angel of Summer rides in a chariot of the South Wind, on wheels that are noiseless. These creative forces are silent and secret forces. Quietly the violet and arbutus unfold beneath the old leaves. Silently these unseen fingers embroider the carpet of the earth with gold and blue. Soon all pastures will wave with grass and all meadows with corn. When at last the voice of the harvester is heard in the land the overflowing granaries will represent the secret and invisible work of One who comes to make all things beautiful and ripe in their time!

VIII

MAN'S GREATEST NEED

"I am come that they might have life, and that they might have it more abundantly."—JOHN x: 10.

WHAT all the world is seeking is life,—life, life, more life—rich, creative life. Now and then a man appears alive to his finger tips, a man who never tires, whose enthusiasm never wanes, as apostle, patriot, reformer, teacher—a man glowing like some planet that sparkles with ten thousand effects. Once in a century we behold one of these vitalised men, a spiritual dynamo, some Paul, flinging off laws, reforms, martyrdoms, and then riding into the sky, perchance, in a chariot of flame. What man wants is life physical, and that means abounding health, passion for work, an eager longing for such new days to come with opportunity for productive industry. Men want life intellectual, and that means a hungry mind, constant growth, increasing culture, a consciousness of being fully equal to any emergency. Man wants life for his affections, and that means an increasing capacity for friendship and loyalty to those we love, with power to keep our friendships in repair. Man wants life spiritual, and that brings the gift of peace, freedom from worry, full power to rise victorious over all disasters and trouble. The secret of happiness and success is in a deep uprising life, rushing forth in exterior service. What we call failure is the consciousness that there is a wide gap between our ambition and our performance.

What is the remedy? Watkinson has a beautiful statement: "Give that despairing musician an atom of Mozart's melodious brain; that halting poet a spark of Shakespeare's fire, that struggling painter a nerve of Turner's colour sense, that stammering orator a little of Demosthenes' tongue, and bitter failure will be at an end; there will be no more exhausting difficulty and delay, only the intoxicating sense of mastery, progress and delight." More life in the learner is what is needed, and then every difficulty is vanquished and every aspiration fulfilled." Now that is the secret of Christ's mission—He comes to give life—rich, creative life. Concerning the great missionaries, prophets and heroes, let us say, "Christ was in them, the mainspring of their energy, the hope of their glory."

With reference to this word "I come to bring life," Matthew Arnold once said, "There is a power in the world, not ourselves, that makes for righteousness." What is called modern civilisation is based upon that unseen power that is not ourselves, but that loans its almightiness to man's littleness. Today, every man is one hundred man power. How? Through "the power that is not ourselves." Today our average income per family is two thousand dollars a year. Through what force? Through the power not ourselves that makes for property. The workman's hand strikes a blow of one hundred pounds, while the unseen power of electricity through a triphammer strikes a blow of ten tons. Man's leg walks four miles an hour, while, through an invisible power, that airplane makes one hundred miles an hour, crossing forests, rivers, plains, two mountain ranges, and reaches the Pacific Ocean in about twenty-seven hours. Man's voice carries to several thousand people, but through the new wireless and the power not ourselves man's words reach several millions. Little wonder that man is called by John a son of God, able now to think God's thoughts out after Him; now with a little reed measuring yonder Milky Way; now weighing distant stars, foretelling their movements, weighing their masses. Man seems approaching, by swift steps, an era when all things in the heavens above and the earth beneath, and even the waters under the earth, shall bow down in His presence, and, like well-trained servants, fulfill His will. But how is it that man turns poisons into medicines and foods? Why, through a power not ourselves, as God progressively loans man's intellect parts of His omniscience; loans man's weakness portions of His omnipotence; loans man's brief years the gift of His eternal life. Not otherwise Jesus progressively gives life and vitality to the nerve of religious sensation; gives a wider vision to man's spiritual optic nerve; gives the love of holiness to man's selfishness. Something transformed that false Jacob into the Prince of Israel. Plainly God met Jacob unexpectedly in the desert. Some great upheaval transformed Saul into Paul. Plainly the life of God was poured into the soul of Saul, making all things new. This word, "I am come to bring life," explains the appearance of great men, the dawn of new eras, the rise of new liberties, the social upheavals that have overthrown ancient abuses, and helped make all things new.

It is comparison and contrast that gives the sense of value and ranks world leaders. Some great religious teachers came interesting themselves in institutions, traditions or manners. Confucius came with a cut-and-dried system of reverence to parents, loyalty to yesterday, and when a hundred years had passed paralysis had fallen upon the creative faculty of the Chinese and made progress a baseless fabric of a dream. Moses came building a tabernacle, planning synagogues, developing rituals and sacrifices. Buddha came digging a chasm between classes and annihilating sensitiveness of feeling, delicacy of emotion, while the heaven he promised was "unconsciousness." Moses built a synagogue—not Jesus. Mohammed founded a mosque—not Jesus. Buddha taught self-immolation, and progressive hardening of the heart—not Jesus. Jesus never built a single church, He never wrote a line or a sermon, He never polished a single creed or litany, He never ordained a single priest or bishop. He came pouring life into the soul of each individual and then left that individual to express himself. Each temperament wrote its own creed, each race wrote its own litany, each tribe developed its own polity and form of government.

What the sun does depends upon the soil and seed. The sun falls on the prairies of Minnesota and the soil answers with wheat. The sun falls on the soil of the South and the soil answers with cotton. The sun falls on the fields of Cuba and Cuba answers with sugar. The sun says to the violet, "Here is abundance; take what you will," and the violet takes a little light and returns perfume; just as the oak takes much light and returns ship-timber. Not otherwise Christ came bringing life as the summer making sun. His light fell upon Wittenburg, and Luther answered with his Bible. The light fell on Geneva and Calvin answered with the *Institutes of Theology.* His light fell on England and Wesley answered with the Freedom of Choice. The light fell on this new world and Jonathan Edwards answered with his *Freedom of the Will,* just as Beecher answered with a statement of the love of God. And now Japan is founding a Japanese Christian Church, but that church will have a Japanese creed, Japanese hymns and a Japanese order of church government. It is this disinterested "Life" given to all races and peoples that makes inevitable a difference in theologies, forms of government and worship. There is one glory of the flowers and another glory of the grains, and another glory of the trees, but the sun is one and the same. Not otherwise different churches have their own forms of excellence, but derive their precious qualities from the same overruling God, and the common Master of us all. Differences of temperament explain the divergencies in creeds.

It is this inrushing rich, creative, divine life, given freely, that brings the disciple immunity to temptation and sin. Scientists tell us that the air is always filled with the germs of every known disease. From time to time some plague-stricken ship drops anchor in one of our harbours and the health authorities become alarmed and the people panic-stricken. Quarantine rules are established; ships are disinfected and bedding in the cabins is burned. Every precaution is taken lest the plague spread. But useful as these barriers are it still remains true that the best safeguard against the deadly fever or plague is plenty of good sleep, abundance of nourishing food, exercise, and a mind free from worry. Drummond defines death as "the point where old cells are in the majority and break down faster than new cells can be built up." For six hours the tide comes in, then comes a critical moment when the tide barely holds its own, and then it slowly begins to ebb. Oftentimes we hear sailors saying concerning one who is desperately sick, "He will go out with the tide." This explains the reason why physicians at the front never stopped telling the nurses that their salvation was in building new cells faster than old ones break down.

The best way to keep the weeds down is to sow the newly-ploughed soil with wheat or oats. It is the shade of the new oats and wheat that holds in check the weeds. The mere absence of thorns and thistles through the negatives of Moses involves starvation. Jesus began anew where the negatives of Moses stopped, and He rushed on to achieve the positives: Thou shalt love, thou shalt hope, thou shalt trust and thou shalt serve. The inrushing life of God forces back the old life of selfishness and sin. The life of God was in Livingstone, and he loved kindness, purity and self-sacrifice. One day Henry Morton Stanley fled from a poor, diseased creature lying beside the path in the forest, but Livingstone picked up the sufferer, carried him to the spring, bathed his body, cleansed the wounds, nursed the wounded one back to health again. Light is an antiseptic for material germs, while love and trust are the great medicines of our spiritual therapeutics.

In bringing this new life Jesus released certain latent and unsuspected powers in man. In his essay on the duty of performing the impossible, and realising tasks quite beyond man's strength and wisdom, Professor James insists that there are whole strata of undeveloped faculties in the human soul. James believed that every man could double his working capacity, increase his efficiency, and achieve as a man deeds attributed to the sons of God. He tells us about men lost in the desert, whose last atom of strength was exhausted—men who had fallen unconscious upon the sand, yet in stumbling upon a dying woman or child, the traveler's intellect and will were startled and they began to draw upon the substratum of energy and go on untired, carrying burdens quite undreamed of hitherto. He speaks of soldiers, unconscious through sheer exhaustion and too weak to lift a finger, but when some one shouts into the man's ear the story of the new peril, suddenly the tired man revives, opens the door into a new chamber of strength, calls forth hidden energies and strides forward as fresh as if he had never heard of tire.

In California the upper stratum of oil-bearing sand is exhausted. Derricks scattered about were pulled down and a landscape hitherto unsightly recovered to beauty. Some scientists believed that there might be a second, underlying, oil-bearing stratum of sand, and the new borings brought gushers, and now, after being exhausted a second time, the oil men of California explored nearly a mile in depth and opened up still newer fields, and today, out of those deep-lying, strangely hidden strata, California is producing more oil riches than any other country whatsoever. Jesus believed in man. "Stretch forth thy hand," He said to the cripple with the shrivelled arm. Once the man knew that it was his duty to perform the impossible he tried to obey, and so won back his health. The shock of the new creative life flowing from a new graft into an old stalk holds Burbank's theory of producing new flowers, new melons, new fruits, new trees, a new human race, and a new world. "I am come to give life," and that means that the ambitious boy can grow. "I am come to give life," and that means that it is always better farther on. How wonderful the opportunity of the next generation!

How easily man can double his working capacity and his efficiency! The manufacturer widens his drainage area to get a deeper and more powerful current to pound upon his turbines. The engineer increases his voltage that he may widen the walls of the world room into which he is speaking. What a coward was John, following afar off! How timid Peter, how repeated and diverse the denials of the disciples! Then Jesus drew near and laid His hands upon these young disciples and poured the life of God into their souls. And immediately they rose in the spirit of heroes. Always the method was the life of God pouring into the soul of the twelve, then the twelve or fifteen touched the three thousand, and poured the life stream into them; then the three thousand put their hands upon forty thousand, and became the channel of still onrushing life; the forty thousand have soon communicated life into a million, and the million unto three millions, and then suddenly Jesus was on the throne of the Cæsars. Personal contact of disciples, having the life of God in their souls, changed the souls of others. Today, we have over eight hundred million Christians in the world. If this company should organise a forward movement we could easily evangelise the sixteen hundred millions of the human race within this generation. This task of redeeming the world is the task of the pew and not alone of the pulpit. Every one of you must be a channel for the life of God, received on the one side and communicated to your brethren on the other. Every one of you must give an account unto God for the condition of your church, your city, and your commonwealth. Do not at your peril ask for this divine gift and then try and hoard it for yourself. Eternal life is kept by being given away. The disciple grows by serving and sacrificing. Physical growth comes through good food, exercise and sleep, and spiritual growth comes by praying for the poor, and loving the unfortunate and serving the unhappy. To be bread to the hungry, to be light to the darkened, to be life to those who sit in the region and shadow of death is henceforth your mission—your duty, and also your opportunity!

It is this principle that explains the occasional disciple who is carried up to apostleship. There is an immeasurable difference between a disciple of Christ and an apostle of Christ. There were five hundred disciples, there were only twelve who became apostles. These hundreds were at peace with God and their own souls, and went tranquilly across the years, but there were a few apostles who borrowed God's spiritual omnipotence, and they went out through the world on a spiritual crusade, breaking down tyrannies, destroying social crimes, turning the whole world of ignorance and sin upside down. A disciple is a pupil, studying. An apostle is a workman, who has passed from learning to achievement. For three years the five hundred were disciples before Christ's death, and they were content to remain disciples all the rest of their lives. But there were a few who felt that three years was long enough for discipleship. After that they stretched up their hands and plucked the sword of omnipotence out of the hand of God, a sword red with insufferable wrath against sin, and went forth to slay iniquity. Water is always water, you say. By no means. The raindrops are water, lying in the quiet little pool, or in Lake Erie. But the energy of Lake

Erie is latent and unreleased. Now let the water of the lake pour over Niagara Falls, and water suddenly becomes dynamic and apostolic, lighting distant villages, working distant factories, carrying burdens for tired workmen. Thus the truth of Christ was a latent and static truth in the five hundred disciples, who were content to be redeemed themselves, but it was dynamic truth in Paul, who went forth to reform, in Peter, who looked upon every rock as a pulpit into which he could climb to evangelise; in James, who went forth with tireless energy to care for the widow and the orphans; in John, who went forth among the turbulent, warring multitudes, to whisper to each combatant,—"love is of God." It is this spiritual energy of God that changes a disciple into an apostle.

History is full of these occasional men who attempt impossible things and plans, and were successful in their exploits. Every man is under an obligation to perform the impossible. His duty is always greater than his ability. When the mother stands the child one year old up against a wall, and commands the child to walk, it is impossible for the child to walk, and yet it is the child's duty. The mother makes a temporary loan of her strength to a child that is attempting the impossible, and the child succeeds, just as God makes a temporary loan of His omnipotence to William the Silent, to Garrison the emancipator, to Livingstone the missionary, and to Booth the reformer. With finite power apostles perform infinite deeds. With human faculties they work divine achievements. Manhood is carried up to the nth power, through the influence of omnipotence. It is an acorn's duty to lift a thousand hogsheads of water into the air during a single summer. Just because each day the little oak plantlet attempts the impossible, the earth at the root and the sun upon the bough enable the oak to achieve that miracle. Now that vegetable fact shadows forth the spiritual impossibilities going on about us every day.

This principle explains the singular influence of some occasional people in the community. There are a few people who seem to have an influence entirely disproportionate to their mental gifts, to their culture or their property. Quietly and unobtrusively they go about, doing their work day by day; and yet, they carry a warm summery climate with them, and the roses and lilies of faith and hope spring up about their feet as they walk up and down the streets. To the few who know them best, they seem miracle workers. With the passing years this power to transform their fellows increases with the waning of their physical strength. Where others grope, they see clearly. Putting out their hands they lead the blind into a path that is henceforth flooded with light. Sometimes they stand in silence, with fingers upon the lips, as if they heard from afar the faint but clear music, rolling in from God's rich sky. And listening, lo, their companions whose ears have hitherto been deaf, suddenly begin to catch the first faint notes of that melody so piercingly sweet.

These who have borrowed God's strength, go forth to those whose hands have dropped the tool, and suddenly the tired worker finds his yoke easy and his burden light. These occasional people differ from the multitudes that throng and press about us, just as Shakespeare differs from a peasant boy. Just as Raphael differs from a paint grinder, just as Christopher Wren differs from a child building block houses. Now how shall we explain them? The greatness of these occasional men and women is the greatness of God in them. The inventor uses the physical forces of God. These gentle disciples do all things through Christ who doth strengthen and make the soul equal to any emergency. Tomorrow, oh, man and woman! thou shalt come to the parting of the ways. Tomorrow will bring an impossible burden, but tomorrow will also bring the will to act upon God's offer to loan you His infinite wisdom and power, against a critical hour, big with destiny for all you love!

In these days when men are talking about the influence of the Church in the community, this principle assumes singular importance. One half of us is talking about equipment, tools, kindergartens, social settlements, clubs, gymnasiums, while the other half is talking about the enduement of power, and the divine tides coming in upon the soul of man. It is as if one man should look at the electric bulb and say, "We need better electric fixtures," while the other man looks at the dynamo in the basement, and remembers only "the invisible current." The central fact is that for light and heat we need both more power and better achievements. The new era means new social devices, better physical life, higher wages, juster laws, a diffusion of all good things, but it means also and primarily the life of God in the soul of man. The relation between the Church and the world is the relation between the sun and the tropics and arctics. God warms the flood of waters at the tropic centre, and the great circular movement begins. The warmed waters and the Gulf current of air starts north toward Labrador and England, and the cold Arctic current and air starts south toward the glowing tropic centre to have the chill of death taken away. Then, when the cold is made warm and quick, it starts north itself, to bring life to the very regions from which once it had its death, while the warm Gulf stream that is now chill and cold turns south again to the warm brooding of the sun above.

So the movement under the law of circularity goes ever on, in God's physical world, as a perpetual symbol of the life of the soul that is warmed by the love of God. Filled with the compassion of Christ, the man-God, goes out during the week into the street chilled by selfishness and frozen with sin, to pour the rich tropic tides of love and compassion upon a winter-clad world. It is the life of God that releases the frozen roots and the chilled seeds, to their summer's growth; it is the spirit of God that is warmth, release, growth, life, to the frozen hearts of men. It is this brooding life and love of God, that brings summer to the soul and makes faith and hope indigenous. What man needs is to be carried up to the nth power of influence and personal worth. Borrowing, therefore, God's physical energy as an inventor; having multiplied each average man by a hundred men, through the energies of electricity, let us remember above all that we may have the infinite strength of God to help us bear life's burdens, conquer its temptations, and fulfill its tasks, until we make the earth to be once more an Eden garden, a veritable heaven of righteousness and peace.

IX

KEEPING FAITH WITH OUR FATHERS

"*Keep that which is committed to thy trust.*"—I TIM. vi: 20.

IN his book of courage Carlyle calls the roll of the heroes of the nations. Phocion is the hero of Athens, Julius Cæsar of Rome, Robert Bruce of Scotland, while Cromwell stands for England and Washington for America. Not otherwise Paul is the hero of the Christian faith—a hero who stands forth supreme, with the second man a score of leagues behind. There will be a hundred Washingtons and Cromwells born before there is another Paul. He was an author, and his *Ode of Love* and his argument upon Immortality are the most quoted and best loved things in literature. He was an orator, and by sheer force of genius he vanquished hostile mobs, talked the stones out of his enemies' hands and talked hate out of their hearts. One day, standing with his left hand chained to the right hand of his jailer, Paul addressed his judge and King Agrippa, and before his plea was completed he had transformed enemies into friends!

Paul was also a theologian and philosopher. Today, if he should return to earth, he would have a right to say to Augustine, "This is my *City of*

God," and to Calvin, "These are my *Institutes of Religion,"* and to Hamilton, "This is my *Republic of God."* Saul was born in a rich man's house, and from childhood was accustomed to ease and luxury. He was educated in a great literary center, and was the favourite pupil of Gamaliel, the teacher. He was the most learned rabbi in the Jewish synagogues, and despite his youth, and the force of tradition, he was elected a member of the Sanhedrim. Gifted with a fiery nature, and untiring zeal, when the new faith began to spread, Saul flung himself with the fury of a tornado upon the band of disciples. He organised a mob and helped zealots stone to death Stephen. With another group he mobbed the home of James and flung the disciple from a second-story window, and so killed the brother of Jesus. Like Torquemada with his rack and thumb-screw and blazing faggot, Saul's hate grew more and more, feeding upon its own fury.

Having heard that a handful of disciples had found an asylum in Damascus, Saul journeyed northward, breathing forth slaughter and penalty. Upon the road to Damascus he saw the heavenly vision, and was at first terrified, then awakened, and finally transformed. Going into the deserts he remained for three years studying the Old Testament prophecies concerning the coming of the Son of Man and the Saviour of the world. He returned to Jerusalem to tell his story before the Sanhedrim. Then began a most dramatic career. He came to know the inside of every prison of the cities about the Mediterranean. Five times he was arrested and convicted of attacking the gods, now of the Greeks and now of the Romans. Five times he was flogged with whips, receiving thirty-nine stripes, and three times he was beaten with rods. Once he was stoned, and left for dead in the streets of Lystra. Thrice also he suffered shipwreck, and once he was a night and a day in the great deep. He suffered perils of robbers, perils in the wilderness, perils in the city, perils among spies and traitors, until at last he achieved a martyr's death, and has a place among "the Immortals."

His words were the words of a hero, for heroism means three things, an unselfish and disinterested spirit, a sincere and pure heart, and a practical common sense method of activity. His last words are revelatory of his true greatness. Bacon said, "Men are not worth the trouble I have taken for them." D'Annunzio said, "Italy is not worth dying for." Turner believed that he "gave society a loaf, and received a stone." Horace Greeley said, "Fame is a vapour, those who praise today will curse tomorrow." A multi-millionaire dying, the other day, whispered, "Is my will all right?" But Paul did not care a straw for gold, nor office, nor fame, nor pleasure, and his last words were, "I have kept the faith." Over and over again he exclaimed, "I have fought a good fight, I have finished my course, *I have kept the faith*."

Heroism is contagious. Fortitude, faith and self-sacrifice spread like wildfire. That is why one great man can save a city, transform a generation, or civilise a state. Heroism appeals to a certain adventurous note in youth. On Commencement Day the richly dressed advocate of some corporation stretches forth his hand, and calls young graduates to the paths of ease and office and luxury, and the great majority give immediate response. His call is in vain. Young men, who represent unique gifts, will decline the bribes and fill their ears with wax against the song of the siren. Then comes some Stanley, saying, "I want to cross Darkest Africa, along the line of the Equator. It is foul with miasm, full of pestilence, holds forests and jungles, with wild beasts and serpents and poison vipers." Now that appeal to the spirit of adventure with the peril of death will be responded to by ten times as many young men as Stanley can use.

It is this that explains Garibaldi's soldiers when he called them to almost certain death. Now the story of Paul's heroism traveled all around the towns and cities that looked out upon the Mediterranean. For a little time the new faith escaped observation. The attitude of Imperial Rome was one of scorn for a leader whose birthplace was a stable. During that quiet interval the young Faith struck its roots down and pushed out its boughs. First of all, peasants, slaves and gladiators went over to the new faith. Then the soldiers became interested. One day the patricians in the palaces awakened to the new faith and then the Emperor decided to stamp out the Christian superstition. He flung upon the devoted disciples the thunderbolts of Rome. Spies secured evidence by attending the secret midnight meetings of the disciples, and soldiers, like a ring of fire, closed in on the intrepid band. Some were driven into the amphitheatre, where wild beasts were let loose upon them. Nero ordered many a youth and maiden bound to stake and covered with straw, oil and pitch, and used them as torches for his garden parties.

The fury of the Emperor was beyond all words. Many a St. Sebastian was bound to a tree and made a target for flaming arrows; many a Perpetua supported her dying father, at the risk of her own limbs and life. Did anyone falter? "Remember Paul." Did some tender boy shiver at the flash of the sword of an executioner? "Think of Paul and his example." What is the explanation of the early Church's victory in its conflict with the power of Rome? The heroic spirit of Paul lighted the sacred flames of faith and heroism in the young disciples and their flame leaped from altar to altar, and town to town! The blood of the martyrs became the seed of the Church, and finally the heroism of Paul won the victory.

But the hero who is willing to die for a cause is a man who has found a cause worth dying for. Brave deeds do not come by chance. Get your Beatrice—Dante is inevitable. Get your clover field, and do not worry about the honey bees, they will come. Get your supreme faith—that faith will evoke heroes to defend it. The difference between the pliable, plastic, wavering Faint-Heart and this granite man, Paul, is that Paul had found a treasure worth fighting for. Fortunately, he stated his faith in terms simple as sunshine, yet as sharply defined as the outlines of a mountain. Only when we place Paul's speech before Agrippa beside the argument of Demosthenes, in his own defense, or a speech of Fox or Sheridan before Parliament, or Fisher Ames against the British Governor, do we realise what really great eloquence is. "Then King Agrippa said unto Paul: 'Thou art permitted to speak for thyself,'" and Paul stretched forth his hand and answered for himself: "I think myself happy' King Agrippa, because I shall answer for myself this day before thee, touching all the things whereby I am accused of the Jews; especially because I know thee to be expert." (What a sure touch is that! How widely does Paul swing open the gate of intellectual hospitality! In that moment he gave sops to the dog Cerberus that guarded the gate into the citadel of the soul of Agrippa and quieted the monster.) "In all customs and questions which are among Jews; wherefore, I beseech thee to hear me patiently. My manner of life from my youth up is known to all the Jews. After the straitest sect of our religion I lived a Pharisee. Now I stand and am judged by the hope of the promise made of God unto our fathers."

By that one stroke Paul, as if by a touch of magic, made Moses and Abraham, and Jacob the prince, David the poet, and Isaiah the prophet, suddenly descend from the clouds and stand beside him, until the very genius of the Hebrew religion seemed to be breaking into voice upon Paul's lips when he said: "For which hope's sake, of the final victory, of the law and the prophets, King Agrippa,

I am now accused by the sons of fathers who themselves kindled this hope within me. And now, O King Agrippa, why should it be thought a thing incredible with you that God should raise the dead? Did not Job declare that he knew that his Redeemer liveth, and that at the last day he would carry away upon his shoulders the gates of death and set man free?"

And then Paul showed Agrippa the king and Festus the governor that every promise in the Hebrew law and prophets had been fulfilled in the Teacher of Galilee. It was a very simple faith—God is our Father, men who have worshipped Him as the Unknown may now see the veil removed and behold His face of light, and hear His words of love, and lean upon arms that are everlasting in moments when the earth reels beneath the feet of the pilgrim and the fog chokes his throat. Paul revealed God as the all-suffering God, as the great-breasted Father, ever abroad by night and day upon His mission of recovery; a God who was calling all His children upward toward wisdom and knowledge, toward love and immortality. These simple faiths were as clear as the stars and as brilliant. They were as solid as the mountains and as enduring. From this supreme faith in principles Paul borrowed his courage, his endurance, his unyielding hope of ultimate victory.

Where were the hidings of power in this hero who, single-handed, assaulted kingdoms, overthrew fortresses of superstition and laid the foundations of a new world? The answer is near at hand. Paul's greatness was rooted in a personal experience of the heavenly vision that he saw on the way to Damascus. He went everywhither telling the story of what his own eyes had seen, what his own ears had heard, and what his heart had felt. The fires of conviction dwelt in his words as heat dwells in the sunbeam and, passing through a sun-glass, sets wood on fire. Other men thought, Paul knew. Other men dreamed, Paul had seen and heard. In every crisis, before the scholars of Athens, the mob in Ephesus, the Sanhedrim in Jerusalem, the rulers in Rome, he had but one story: "I went to Damascus as an enemy, and breathed forth slaughtering and hate. Suddenly, while I was in the way, a light shone forth, and I found that I loved the disciples, whom hitherto I had hated. Also I revolted from cruel leaders in Jerusalem whom hitherto I had admired and obeyed." Then for thirty years that Jesus whom he loved and served stood beside him as his personal leader, Saviour, Guide and Friend.

His every argument began with this: "I have not been disobedient unto the heavenly vision." Not otherwise every new era for the Christian Church has been ushered in by some man who has seen a vision and has not been disobedient thereto. Witness Augustine, redeemed by a vision out of the mire and pit of the effeminate, luxurious and sensual city of Rome. Witness Martin Luther in Rome slowly climbing the steps upon his knees, for whom the light of divine love flamed forth! Witness John Wesley, kneeling to pray and suddenly conscious that something had happened in his heart, and that something was like the stealing of a sunbeam into a room and falling across the page of an open book. Witness Harriet Beecher Stowe telling the story of Uncle Tom and Aunt Chloe as she had seen them in the little cabin in the old Kentucky home. Witness the books of Jonathan Edwards, that represent the memory of a great spiritual experience that enriched a thousand pages of writing. In the self-same way the sermons of Henry Ward Beecher, Horace Bushnell and Phillips Brooks are all the simple story of the way of God with a son, now in the forests near Indianapolis, now in the student's room in the seminary at Alexandria. Paul knew what that heavenly vision had done for him. Joyously he welcomed the heavenly vision and hastened to obey it, and rapturously he told his story. What he had seen with his own eyes and felt wits his own heart he declared unto men. The greatness of this hero was the greatness of God in his heart.

Paul's most dramatic appeal was made unto his own countrymen. He was not only the most learned and the most brilliant, but the bravest rabbi of his time. The faith of Paul's fathers was nearly two thousand years old. That ancient faith burst into the life and teachings of Jesus as naturally as the root bursts into full flower and fruit. It was a noble faith—the faith of Abraham, Isaac and Jacob, of Elijah and David, of Isaiah and Malachi. It was as massive as a cathedral, as enduring as the living oak of Hebron, as rich in memories and traditions as Westminster Abbey, holding the dust of kings and scholars for hundreds of years. Not the threshold of the Parthenon was so sacred as the threshold of that beautiful temple, where Jesus, the tallest figure in the long line of prophets, stood, with His outstretched arms, and exclaimed, "Oh, Jerusalem! Jerusalem! thou that killest the prophets and stonest them that are sent unto thee, how often would I have gathered thee as a hen gathereth her chickens under her wings, and ye would not." And the prophet of Nazareth was their prophet—the Jews—and the greatest of their prophets. Moses said, "Thou shalt not," Jesus said not, and "Thou shalt not"—"Thou shalt hope, thou shalt love, thou shalt trust!" When Moses had slain all the foul weeds in the garden of the soul, Jesus planted the roses and the lilies, with corn for man's hunger. Moses said, "An eye for an eye and a tooth for a tooth"; Jesus said, "Thou shalt love thine enemies, for God maketh His sun to rise on the evil and the good, and sendeth rain upon the just and the unjust." The law and the prophets said, "The wages of sin is death," but Jesus said, "God is love and has come to seek and to save that which is lost."

What kindness to little children! What pity to the outcast! What tenderness to the publican and sinner! How wondrous that moment when He lifted the rags from the beggar, and looked up at the stars and whispered a great hope. It was His hand that opened the rift in yonder sky. What a word is this that falls through the silent air: "Let not your heart be troubled. In My Father's house are many mansions." The Great Nazarene belonged to the Jews, and they should have claimed and followed Him! That high priest, Caiaphas, should have been the first bishop of the Christian Church in Jerusalem. Paul should have been the first evangelist ever sent out by the Sanhedrim. Annas should have flung himself between Jesus and the mob with the Roman soldiers and Pilate, and shouted, "You shall not lift Him to this cross! You shall not touch one hair of His head while any Hebrew rabbi lives!" And Handel's *Messiah* might have been, and should have been, the symphony of the Hebrew. The Jew has a great stake in the laws of Moses, and the philosophy of Kant and Hegel; in the music of Beethoven and Mendelssohn. But his greatest stake, and his largest investment is in the law and the prophets that are root and trunk, that burst into flower and fruit in Christ's evangel of love.

There cannot be, there must not be, any hatred between any Jew and any Gentile. Of late, during these dark days, one has many times wondered why noble Hebrew scholars, patriots and lovers of their fellow-men have not claimed the Nazarene as the tallest flower that ever grew in their Hebrew garden. As the mightiest tree that ever unfolded its boughs and branches in God's divine Eden! As the supreme voice that rings through all the synagogues, calling men not only to law but to love and mercy. Jesus brought the world a new thought of God, freedom, love and immortality. Those who should first have lifted the trumpets upon their lips were Jewish musicians, those first to wave the triumphal banners should have been Jewish people; those who lighted the flames of the sacred fires should have been the hands of Hebrews. The pierced hands of the Nazarene prophet never made a wound, though He healed many; never extinguished a torch, though He kindled many a light to shine into the dark night; never plucked hope out of a human heart, though He planted many an aspiration.

And the first people on earth to walk in His triumphal procession should have been the Hebrews, walking in the vanguard, while the rest of us followed as captives in His triumphal procession, up the hills of time. Sooner or later the mists will pass, the clouds will dissolve.

Many mistakes have been made on both sides during the last thousand years; many crimes have been committed, but the Nazarene was right—across the gory battlefields of time, above all the din and tumult of the struggle, there rises one clear voice saying, "Let not your heart be troubled." Sooner or later love will be victorious over hate, liberty will conquer oppression, God will arise and by mercy subdue all His enemies. And first among His followers in that great day of this immortal hope shall be Paul, the brilliant Hebrew rabbi, the noblest hero and the whitest saint of all the centuries!

But there is a faith of the fathers, the Republic and its free institutions, that must be kept. Each week brings fresh revelations of traitors who have betrayed the faith of the founders of our Republic. In Western Pennsylvania one hears about the burning of four million dollars' worth of buildings—school houses, churches, homes, stores and farmers' granaries. Is this a secret organisation whose members believe, as do Bolsheviks, that everything must be burned to the ground, and then built up again by believers in the Soviet form of government? Anarchists? Yes. Nihilists? Yes. Bolsheviks? Yes. But, essentially, men who live from the hand to the stomach, men who no longer believe in any God, or future life, or responsibility for the deeds done in the body.

But how could it be otherwise? Look at these foreigners, after a week at Ellis Island. Mark the revolution in the physical conditions of the island, with buildings kept spotlessly clean, playgrounds for children, a nursery for the little ones, and cleanly wards for the sick. But scarcely have these immigrants left Ellis Island than they receive in various languages the poison of anarchy and revolution which is instilled into the mind and heart. We have a daily paper in New York published in English, and also in German. The sentiments in English represent vague anti-Americanism, and the sentiments in the foreign language represent treason to this Republic. Scarcely have these foreigners landed at the railroad stations, than they receive a card published in six languages containing essentially these statements: "Immigrants, remember that this is a capitalistic government. Remember it is a dirty and a rotten government, where the capitalist will exploit your life. The only way you can get a job is to join a radical society or union Join some revolutionary society, and help us overthrow this wicked, capitalistic government."

But what men sow they reap. Sow wheat—you

reap sheaves. Sow thistles, you reap thistles. Sow sparks, you reap conflagrations. Sow hatred of this Republic, you reap revolution. There is one race in this country that, to every one crime committed by the native American, commits ten crimes per thousand citizens. There is another foreign people, new in this country, that commits eight crimes where a native American commits one. This Republic cannot exist, half American and half alien. Either Americanism must expel anti-Americanism, or the anti-American sentiment will Bolshevise our people and destroy our Republic. Soon for all parents and patriots and teachers, the end shall come, just as Paul knew that his execution was set for the following day. In reviewing his life, he exclaimed, as he anticipated meeting Jesus, "I have kept the faith!" But have you kept the faith of the American school? Have you flattered men to win their votes, and debauched the voters of your city? Has your service been venial, selfish? Have you lowered the ideals of patriotism? Have you been what is called a practical politician? Have you helped elect men as judges, using money, because later on they could be influenced to give an occasional decision worth much money to those who paid their election bills? Have you betrayed the Church, the Sunday and the family itself? Many of you are in the afternoon of life's day. Already the shadows are falling lower. Soon the end will come. Be wise while it is yet time. Give yourselves in loyalty to the great convictions. When the end comes, and you go into the great company of immortals, see to it, that in that hour when all noble ancestors are turned toward you, that you are able to lift your hand and say without fear: "I have kept the faith of my country, I have kept the faith of my friends, I have kept the faith of God, and His dear Son, who is the Saviour of the world."

X

THE LOST RICHES OF THE WORLD

"Where moth and rust doth corrupt."—MATT. vi: 19.

THE story of lost riches of past generations makes a most fascinating page in history. For centuries the various races who lived about the Mediterranean accumulated gold, silver and precious stones, and then hid treasure boxes filled to overflowing. Long afterward the Roman emperors looted Carthage and Alexandria, Athens and Corinth, Ephesus and Jerusalem. In the fourth century, Alaric and his Goths heard the story of "The Golden House" and started across the Alps to loot Rome. They found in the treasure house of the Emperor tables of "solid emerald," the Missorium, a dish weighing 2,500 pounds, covered with the richest gems of India. One day Alaric and his men encamped around the walls of Ravenna and waited for the citizens within to starve and die, as wolves wait around the dying buffalo. "What terms will you make?" asked the messenger, of Alaric, and the Goth answered, "All your gold, all your silver, all the best of your precious things, and all your barbarian slaves." "What, then, will you leave us?" asked the envoy. "Your lives," was the scornful answer.

So the citizens bought Alaric off with this ransom: "Five thousand pounds weight of gold in bars, thirty thousand pounds of silver, three thousand bolts of scarlet cloth, four thousand rolls of silk." Long afterward the Arabs captured from Alaric's successor that emerald table, with its three rows of great pearls. What has become of all that treasure? Diamonds are practically indestructible, and so are gold and silver, with rubies and emeralds and sapphires. It is wood and iron and stone that perish. Where are those great nuggets of gold that Solomon brought from Ophir? Where are all the diamonds that were taken out of the white sands of Golconda, from which came the Kohinoor and the Great Mogul? Many of these diamonds, doubtless, are in use today, while upon some of the old gold there may be stamped the image and superscription of a new president or king. When Alaric died, under the walls of Cosenza, twenty thousand Goths turned the river bed into a new channel, and in the old one they set Alaric, armed and sitting upright upon his horse, and covered with gold and jewels, and then they turned back the river into its old bed. To this day no man knows where Alaric lies or whether the treasure was washed out to the sea or has sunken in slime and mud. Doubtless vast quantities of these jewels were hidden from time to time, while the few who knew the hiding-place were slain by enemies or perished through plague. The Spaniards alone are believed to have taken several hundreds of tons of silver and of gold out of the storehouses and mines of Peru and Mexico. Dumas makes his greatest novel turn upon the burial of the gold and jewels of an Italian prince, and historians hold that the lost riches of the world were buried by men who lost their lives rather than give up the precious secret.

Great riches must abound whenever youth is not neglected. "Spread wide thy mantle while the gods rain gold," is the Persian proverb. That noble sage looked upon youth as a rich mine of gold. All things are possible during the days when the heart is young. Youth has the physical strength to grasp the tool, to open the furrows and sow the seed, to master the chisel, the pen or brush, and youth also has a vast realm of futurity in which to toil. Time is the stuff out of which the intellect and will build the structure of life and success. In youth, also, the intellect is alert, nimble, and hungry for facts. In youth the memory is quick and sensitive like molten glass that soon hardens into permanent form. In youth, also, ambition for excellence, with passionate aspirations, sweep through the heart with the majesty of a summer's storm. Middle age may mean September, and the period when the soul assembles its harvest, but every harvest field has to be prepared for by a sowing in April, and a cultivation in May and June. A prosperous old age is simply the place where youth assembles the fruitage of its long toil.

Many a successful man has found his last years embittered by the neglect and the follies of his youth. That was a wise and illuminating article published by that author who exclaimed, "Oh! that I could live my life over again and begin anew at twenty-one." The genius of his argument is this: That Nature became the ally of every grain of corn planted, and that land and sea and sky worked while the sower slept, and, working, Nature spent one hundred and fifty days in turning a tiny grain of corn into a tall stalk. "Accumulate in the teens a thousand useful facts and principles that they may grow into a rich harvest when the forties and fifties come." Invested at compound interest, the little treasure, assisted by long time, becomes great wealth. Concerning a poet, Coleridge once said that "No man ever became a singer after he was twenty-one years of age." Coleridge might have extended the principle in such a way as to explain the tragedy of his own career by saying, "No man can live happily and prosperously in middle age who cannot look peacefully and joyously back to his youth." One of the saddest chapters in literature holds the words of that broken-down, Hebrew Crœsus named King Solomon. The memories of his years were full of remorse and bitterness, and he therefore assembled before his thought all the children in his kingdom, and charged them with poignant eloquence to remember their Creator in the days of their youth, lest the evil days come, when maturity and old age have no pleasure in the beauty of the days or the silent majesty of the nights, since prince and peasant alike must give their account unto God.

That youth also loses great riches who neglects adversity and necessity, as teachers of the science of manhood. Many parents spend their whole lives trying to accumulate enough property to release their children from the necessity of thrift, prudence and economy, and so become the unconscious enemies of the very children whom they love as they love life itself. Power to use and to enjoy comes from the power to create the thing possessed. The Greek athlete carried the calf upon his shoulders, and then as the calf grew, he daily lifted the burden to his shoulders, and so at length carried a bullock around the arena. One of the reasons why many a man who falls heir to a fortune is unable to keep the treasure is, that he did not have the strength to produce the riches he could not use.

In New York stands a rich man's house. The owner, a man of twenty-nine, carries eternal youth in his mind and heart. In the great apartment in which he lives are perhaps forty old historic Italian masterpieces. Every one has been verified by Italian and French experts, who have given their entire career to the study of some three or four hundred Italian masterpieces. From his childhood the owner has had this consuming passion for Italian paintings! When he was scarcely five years of age his father fell on evil times and dire misfortune. His mother died when he was about six. The boy sold newspapers, ran errands, and on cold and bitter days slipped into the saloon or store to warm his hands and feet against the chill of winter. Little by little he came to read the faces of men as so many open books. He knew what men were selfish and avaricious; he knew the signs of weakness and cruelty, he knew when men were telling him lies, and also when men's words rang true. In his early teens, wearing the garb of a miner, one day the boy appeared at Andover Academy. All the education he had, had been gained by reading in the light of a candle before breakfast and after dark. When asked if he were ready to take the examinations for entrance he answered that he did not so much as know what an examination was. Noble teachers allowed the boy to enter the class and listen, getting what he could, and within a year this youth was tutoring other boys in his class.

Going to Yale, he founded a little industry, with which he earned enough to carry himself through college. Then came the years in the Philippine Islands, the organisation of a great industry, his selection as president thereof, and finally his elevation to control by one of the great firms in England. Now one part of his income is being used for the support of schools, teachers, physicians, ministers, in the Far East, while the other part is used for the purchase of old Italian masterpieces whenever a great painting comes upon the market, through the exigency of war, for the Italian prince merchant in whose family the painting has been held for several hundred years. What courage in this poor boy! What fortitude! What strength of will! What initiative! No one who knows this youth well can doubt but that he is to have an even larger place in the future financial life of the Republic. An orphan at six, at seven a little waif, drifting through the streets of a mining town in Pennsylvania, in retrospect those twelve years when the boy held heartbreak at bay are seen to have been a school for training his talents. Just as Aladdin went down into a cave to bring up the jewels, so this youth brought his treasure up from poverty, squalour, ignorance and suffering. By wrestling he grew strong and by self-reliance he made himself great.

Men who think meanly of themselves and their own gifts lose great riches. The ancient races emphasised the pride of ancestry. The Hebrew king traced his blood back to a noble ancestor, and claimed to be the descendant of Abraham, Isaac and Jacob, just as the men of Athens boasted that they were descended from the goddess Pallas Athene, or as the Romans claimed that they were descended from that divine parent, Æneas. Of the twelve disciples, the most gifted was John. That beloved youth often spoke of his fellow-fishermen as "sons of God." Remembering that wonderful Teacher with whom he lived during three wonderful years, the beloved pupil developed a certain weight of character and influence. At last as he walked through the streets he was as one conscious of the imperial palace from whence he came, and his own divine splendour and origin. Selfishness is an inward looking quality that debases, shrivels, and finally paralyzes the soul, but the spirit of selflessness aiming at service, is an outward looking quality and opens up gateways toward greatness. It was this selflessness that made Lincoln a student by day and night; that made John Bright an investigator of the poverty of the factory classes of England; that made

Charles Dickens turn every whither in search of arguments and weapons against Squeers and Gamp and Bumble, and in defense of poor Smike, doomed to be a drudge and a slave to others. The mission of our earth is to produce great men, who toil tirelessly for wisdom and skill in the art and profession with which they may serve others. Every new era is ushered in for society by a new son of God, who has borrowed divine wisdom from an unseen Father and so comes to walk the earth a true shepherd of multitudes, a true builder of states. Beside every cathedral stands a great architect. Beside every new engine or loom stands a great inventor. Beside every body of law stands some Moses, some Justinian, some Marshall. Society receives its *Principia* from the hand of a great mathematician, its Constitution from the hand of a great statesman. The mission of the State, therefore, is the production of great souls.

Today, as never before, our Government is trying to make parents, physicians, teachers and statesmen realise the importance of a healthier race and a sounder body, as the instrument of a sound mind. Our scientists have perfected the thermometer that tests the temperature of the room. Not otherwise have they completed certain tests of mentality, until we now know to a nicety just how many objects lying upon a table can be remembered by the average normal child of five years, of ten years, of fifteen years or of twenty years. After these ten or twelve tests have been given, the expert will give you the exact mentality of the youth, and show you his place in the scale of life. One of the amazing things in the reports of the physical examinations of six million young men, two million of whom went abroad, two million of whom were drilled at home, and two million of whom were rejected, was the discovery that more than a third of them, with the years of the soldier for the draft, had the mentality of the normal child of eleven years of age.

Now the child of eleven derives its knowledge from seeing and hearing and tasting, as well as from conversation and play. The child of eleven does not think, in the sense of analysing and comparing things that are alike and contrasting things that are different. These physicians discovered that one-third of our people are content to put their hands to the spade or to perform routine work, and are unwilling to disturb their minds with plans for a better tool, a better law or a juster liberty. Now and then, perhaps, some crisis, some violent upheaval may startle the sleeper, as the blast of the trumpet startles the soldier from his slumbers, but it seems certain that millions of our people represent latent treasure, buried riches, resources that will remain in them as gold undug and silver unsmelted. It may be that there is some little congestion in the brain, some nerve, some clog in a hidden vein, some obstruction that inhibits thinking, and makes it certain that for the immediate future at least there will be millions of contented folk, who shrink from mental exertion, physical labour, and all these represent a form of buried riches and hidden treasure.

Whenever love is neglected, whenever friendship is passed by, great riches for society is thrown away. Not many are born with the gift of friendship! Affection is a birth gift from God and one's fathers, just as music is a gift, just as painting, or literary style are gifts, ancestral. Not many Platos! Not many Shakespeares! Paul was a disinterested lover of his fellow-men. With exultant joy he broke the alabaster box of his love upon the head of the gladiator, the slave and the outcast. To a far greater degree Jesus was the universal Lover, who had the enthusiasm of love, the passion for service. Jesus's love for the poor and weak was like that of some Dante for the noble girl, Beatrice; like some master's love for his eager pupil; like some mother's love for a child that has suffered illness or accident. The miracles of Jesus were really bounties and gifts to the heart-broken. Being rich of mind and heart, Jesus gave like a prince, and went up and down the land like a band of music, like a walking oasis, like an organised treasure city, and the gates turned, were open day and night. And above every granary, and storehouse, and library, He wrote these words, "Take what you will." Therefore the common people heard Him gladly, and pressed and thronged about His person to hear His marvelous words. The poor are like the children—they know their friends.

Frienaship is a very delicate blossom. It hides its fragrance like the arbutus. Its perfume is detected before the flower is uncovered. All friendship is an exchange of gifts. The selfish have no friends. Those who give, demanding as much or more in return, are like the frost which falls upon the blossoms to blacken and to blight. It is the friendliness of the clouds bestowing rain that evokes mist from the sea, gladly returning the treasure to the giver. In May, the soil lends food and sap to bough and branch, and in October the boughs return the leaves to refresh the soil and enrich the giver of its own good. Many stand in old age bewildered, wondering why it is that they are unloved and uncared for. Unconsciously they are like a neglected orchard, whose fruit is choked by wild growths and poisoned with moths and ruined by caterpillars, and all because there was no kind hand to care for blossoms and fruit. Alas for the man who wishes friends but who refuses to show himself friendly! Who asks everything and gives nothing! One by one our friends depart, and every day, therefore, new friends must be made, old friendships kept in repair, and through service life must be made rich. That man with his one talent wrapped the gift in a napkin and buried it, and merited the rebuke that Jesus gave.

Much of the treasure of society is lost also through men who are outwardly rich but inwardly poor towards God. All these had no skill in ruling their gold and compelling it to serve. It has often been said that what God thinks of money is set forth in the selfishness of the men to whom He gives it, but this is, sometimes, an unjust proverb. At rare intervals only are the heirs of great wealth able to keep the treasure, much less to increase the fortune. England's laws of primogeniture represent an organised attempt to make it impossible for the son to waste the inheritance that really belongs to his descendants. Nothing is harder to explain than the progressive hardening of the heart and freezing of the sensibilities until a man who in his youth, when he had but little, shared his treasures, yet in his old age clings so tightly to his dollars that you cannot separate him therefrom. Some of these men live and die in the delusion that they at last have solved the problem how to carry wealth on across the River of Death into another world.

But money is of no value unless it works in society as leaven in the meal. To collect and keep money for its own sake, without using it to send one boy to college and another into mission work, without educating the girl in music or teaching, without bearing the burdens of the poor, is as irrational as for a musician to collect millions of sheets of music without taking the trouble to learn how to play; it is as silly as for an artist to collect hundreds of thousands of brushes and tubes of paint without ever beginning a canvas. What if some rich merchant should lay water pipes up the mountain side to a great spring that flows by day and by night, and then, when the water is bubbling at the faucet and the thirsty workmen and the children have brought their cups, what if the old curmudgeon should say, "Get away from here! I have no water for you!" In refusing to fill that cup, he has not saved a drop of water. For when the faucet is shut off, the water rises in the far-off reservoir and overflows and wastes itself on the hillside. Moses told the people that manna was given for one day, while manna hoarded for tomorrow spoiled before the tomorrow came! Thus gold is to be used and not hoarded for later generations. Cicero was right: "Kindness and love makes gold to shine, makes riches splendid."

XI

WHAT IF CHRIST HAD NEVER BEEN?

"And if Christ be not . . . we are of all men most pitiable."—I COR. xv: 17, 19.

SEVERAL authors, with varying skill, have written books on the condition of the world if Christ had never been. Every one is familiar with Jean Paul's dream of the children, coming into the church and sobbing out their sorrow because there is no Christ, and no Christmas, and that all alike are orphans. Henry Rogers wrote a book called *The Eclipse of Faith,* in which he imagines that some powerful hand has wiped the influence of Christ out of civilisation, as some hand wipes the chalk writing from the blackboard of the schoolroom. This brilliant author represents himself as going into his library to discover that every vestige of Christ's life and words has wholly disappeared. He opens his law books, upon the legal safeguards protecting children in the poorhouses, the orphans, the chimney-sweeps, the boys in the coal mines, the poor in tenements, the slaves everywhere, and lo, all these laws have disappeared, leaving paragraphs blank in some law books, with here and there whole pages, and indeed, entire chapters entirely blank, until what is left in the code is meaningless jargon. Alarmed, he turned to his histories of art, and where the *Transfiguration* had been he found a blank page, and to the galleries, but instead of the *Sistine Madonna* of Raphael and the *Ecce Homo* of Guido Reni, and Rembrandt's *Prodigal Son,* with thousands of other masterpieces, he found only empty frames.

Turning to the greatest poems of Dante and Milton, of Wordsworth and Tennyson and Browning, he found nothing but empty leaves with the number of the page at the top. Having long loved architecture with a great passion, his thoughts flew to St. Peter's in Rome, to Milan and Cologne and Westminster Abbey, and lo, nothing remained there but great cellars, for when the Cross went, the cathedrals fashioned in the form of that Cross, perished also. And then it was that Rogers realised that if Christ had never been, the schools, the hospitals, the beautiful philanthropies, the missions, so beneficent in their influence at home and abroad, would all perish, as if shaken down by some cosmic earthquake. Then this lawyer cried out that he would not want to live at all in a world where Christ had never been.

Be the reasons what they may, there are men today, who propose a revolution against Jesus in thought and life. What, if in the stress of a great crisis, representatives of the nations of the earth should meet together, ostensibly to destroy war and organise a universal peace? But when the chairman of the conference begins his opening address, however, everyone notices the cynical look upon his face and the bitter note that has crept into his voice. Perhaps the burden of his argument has to do with the economic wastes of Christian sympathy. He makes a plea against the industrial losses incident to Christ's story of the Good Samaritan. He estimates that our generation would save fifteen to twenty percent by coming out boldly for the anarchistic principle of every fellow for himself and the devil take the hindmost. He urges that the weak have no right to survive and ought to go to the wall; that it is an outrage for the strong to be made unhappy by carrying the burdens of the weak. "Look abroad over the world—everywhere this Galilæan's baneful influence is found. Why should the poorly born not die today, since they must die tomorrow? Why should not this conference declare plainly that Jesus of Nazareth, with His doctrine of love, pity and self-sacrifice, has laid an unbearable burden upon men? The key-word in this crisis," he says, "is revolt. Let us return to Nature, and live as the beasts and birds in the forests live, and die as they die—namely, a natural death, having no regard for these petty dreams of Christian immorality—" And what if this man carries the delegates, and with one voice they shout aloud, "Away with this superstition! Down with these spires!" And what if in the midst of the noise and confusion the twilight should fall and suddenly in the darkness a still, small voice be heard, that in the silence of each heart turns to thunder, "What I have made shall be unmade. It shall be as you have willed. Henceforth the light that was given is withdrawn, and for angels' bread there shall be the apples of Sodom, and for the wine and the nectar of Paradise there shall be what you ask, the dropping of asps and the poison of serpents!"

And what if, going into the streets, these apostates should look with hating eyes upon an altered world? Lifted, now, all the restraints of law! Wild men who through fear and shame had restrained their appetites now suddenly reveal themselves. It is as if harpies and assassins leap from every alleyway upon those delegates, as the mob spirit bursts loose. Then comes the crashing of plate glass windows, the shrieks of night watchmen, the looting of splendid stores and shops, and in the suburbs are flaming houses, and the shrieks of women and the moans of little children, for the beast is let loose, because there is no Christ to stand between the wicked man and his victim. The scene is as dreadful for that great city as if the bells of time had tolled the beginning of eternity, while the great serpent winds his coils about the earth to crush it into nothingness. The noise heard is the crash of falling domes, cathedrals and ministers, with the sound on the pavement of pictures falling from their places, and statues tumbling from their niches, when structures of art and literature and law and reform manifest in architecture, come down in full ruin. It is as if the sun had tumbled from the sky, leaving a black socket.

Of course, if there were no Christ, our civilisation would immediately change. Christendom would go, because there would be no estimating time from the new era, beginning with the day when that beautiful summer civilisation set forth from Bethlehem. Time would doubtless begin with the story of Romulus and Remus. The year would then be 2753, and the dominant power would be the force of that imperial city, of militarism, law and government standing on the banks of the Tiber. Our civilisation would perish and sink into dust with the sinking of the teachings and example of Christ. When we speak of civilisation, we think of our ships, our office buildings, our factories, our great industries, our schools and libraries and churches; but all this is an illusion. What we ought to think about is the ideas, affections and great convictions that have been realised in these material structures.

Suppose that every building in the United States were blotted out, leaving the forests, minerals, grains, fruits unchanged. Now bring in 100,000,000 Mohammedans to take the place of Americans. Soon the ideas of these Turks and Arabs would organise the wood and the iron and stone into mosques, minarets, palaces for the sultans, harems, slave markets, with horsemen armed with spears, planning a raid across the line upon Canada to the north or Mexico to the south. Different ideas coerce metals, forests, stone quarries, into different forms of architecture. All this gorgeous equipage of our civilisation is but an outer show that is as fleeting as the leaf. The thing that abides is the thought, affections and visions of the heart. Therefore, touch the teachings of Jesus at your peril! Destroy Christ's teachings as to His little ones, whose angels behold the face of His Father in heaven, and the orphan asylums, kindergartens and schools would dissolve, like the snowflakes on a river. We trace all granaries, all wheat shocks and sheaves back to that first perfect grain of wheat, in which all harvests were latent. We trace all noble buildings back to the first house. We trace a great river like the Mississippi back to a little spring. And we trace the outer institutions of civilisation back to the teachings of Jesus as to a soul made in the image of God, a soul that must love and serve its brothers and finally give its account unto God.

But if there were no Christ, to whom would the modern man go in the hour when the world reels beneath his feet, when the fog chokes his throat, and he clutches at what Tennyson calls "dust and straw and chaff," where he needs to find the rock? When the thoughtful man gives up that which is good, he expects to obtain something that is better. Will a man leave a stone house in time of storm to seek a frail tent? Man's body must have food, and his anxiety for harvests abides. Man's intellect must have the truth, and more and more he desires books, and thirsts for knowledge and beauty. All these musical instruments found in old museums, beginning with the reed, and the rude strings stretched over the mouth of seashells, and the drums of the medicine man, an ascending series that culminates in the pipe organ, are proofs of man's artistic needs. But what about the passion for righteousness, that deathless longing in the soul of Augustine, conscious of his black sins? that tragic cry of David, calling unto the heavens for pity, forgiveness and cleansing; that muffled sob in the throat of Cicero, when he exclaimed, after the death of his beloved daughter, "Is there a meeting place for the dead?"

When men were starving in Armenia for want of wheat, they substituted grass roots, and when Christianity is gone, men want a substitute. But it cannot be found in Confucius—Confucius has had centuries for his work, and the end is the Chinese Wall, national exclusiveness, polygamy, the parents' right of life and death over an unwelcome female babe, the headsman's axe. Confucius has produced China, and no American will exchange this city for what goes on upon the banks of the Yangste River. Not one of you will, as a substitute, accept the leader of the Brahmins, or the Buddhists. India is a monument of that faith. The English army and government have abolished their Juggernaut car, the burning of the several widows upon the funeral pile of their dead husbands, and many other foul and cruel results of the Indian faith; but Brahminism stands for the caste system and you are Americans, believing in equality. You can have no interest in the harem or the zenana, or the idolatrous orgies, or in the worship of millions of gods or in the goal promised of a "dreamless sleep." You can achieve unconsciousness in a moment by a rope, a pistol, a little cyanide of potassium.

But surely this word unconsciousness is not the last word of a religion by which one can live and die? It is certain also that you will not accept as a substitute the Positivism of Comte, with his three hundred and sixty-five heroes and a new name for each day, to be used as a substitute for Christ and for God. You know, as you read their names—Cicero, Lamartine, Goethe—that the names of these hundreds of men hold a certain admixture of selfishness and vice and meanness and even of crime. Nor can you substitute for Christianity the Agnosticism or Secularism of these teachers of today. Witness Martineau's question: "Will any moonlit form be seen kneeling in their Gethsemanes? Will they rise from prostrate anguish to sublime repose through the prayer, 'Oh, thou Eternal Not Ourselves, that makes for righteousness, let this cup pass from me.' Will any crucified one lose the bitterness of death by crying, 'Oh, Stream of Tendency, into thy hands I commit my spirit?' To the martyr, stoned to death, will any heaven open when he exclaims, 'Great Ensemble of Humanity, receive me?' Will any penitent soul pour out its sorrows to a deaf ideal and shed its passionate tears on an abstraction that cannot wipe them away?" But if there were no Christ, nought else is left save these abstractions. If the wheaten loaf is not, it remains for man to clutch at the fog-bank and feed his hunger upon mist. It is Christ then—or nothing!

If Christ were not, then the human intellect loses its only rational explanation ever given of the problem of suffering and sorrow. To deny the existence of pain is as foolish as to deny an earthquake that destroyed those towns in Japan, or that tidal wave that destroyed Lisbon, or the war that cursed Belgium and France. Grant the existence of summer and its harvests, and we must accept the winter and snow also. Grant the garden, the palm trees and fountains, and we must grant the desert, and the occasional famine. Ours is a world over which, from time to time, troubles sweep like sheeted storms. No man can escape. Genius has sought out many inventions, discovered many secrets, but genius has never built a door that can shut out trouble. Soon or late death robs us of our loved ones. At last comes an era when the grasshopper becomes a burden and all desire fails. Then comes the messenger upon his errand of release and convoy, and comes not for others this time, but for us.

And in the world of selfishness and ignorance and sin Jesus comes into collision with the Pharisees, and Roman governors, and slave owners, and the more unyielding His convictions and ideals, the fiercer the collision. Denial is not enough; mere denial of pain will cure no torture of the soul in its Gethsemane. Then Jesus enters the scene. His message is that sufferings are educatory; that when the summer fails to turn the acid of the grapes to sugar, or sweeten the nuts, the frost completes the transformation; that gold is tried in the fire, and acceptable men in the furnace of adversity; that the self-sacrifice of one hero, with his death, means life and happiness to those who come after; that the greatest souls have come out of great tribulation, from the days of Moses and Paul, with their martyrdom and unaccomplished aims, to the days of Lincoln and Livingstone; that the richness of the soil begins with the glaciers' ice plough; that granite boulders are melted by fire billows, and that slowly, from upheaval, comes harvests and a soil fit for growing the tree of life.

Earth's noblest souls have proven the soundness of Christ's teaching. Witness your own experience. Hours there are when for you everything fails, and doubts come in; but there is one face that shines like a star, the face of your beautiful mother, who came through all the battle of life, gathering sweetness, purity, tenderness and love, and her testimony to the days when she learned in suffering the lessons she later taught, has held you to your work, like an anchor—sure and steadfast. In that hour of transfigured intellect you know that Jesus's philosophy was sound, and His secret sure; that He alone had the clue of the maze, and that therefore you can go on through all the thunder of life's battle, serene in the conviction that whom the Lord loveth He chasteneth, and that He makes all the sons of genius and of goodness to be perfect through suffering. The greatest discovery that our world has ever known was not Columbus' discovery of America, nor Newton's discovery of gravity, nor Franklin's discovery of electricity—none of these things—but the discovery of growth and character and salvation through suffering, through the surrender of the will of man to the Will of God, and the determination to do right though the heavens fall. Christ's simple statement of the mission of sorrow and the sad plight of a world without pain has transformed the world and wrought a new era for the soul, just as the doctrine of Newton brought a new era to astronomy.

But if the world were without Christ men would lose the motive to service and heroism. It was Jesus who made the sum of religion to be service and kindness, its emblem a cup of cold water and its genius to be helpful. The soul is not self-propulsive. All sailing boats need the trade winds. There is no locomotive that does not depend upon some exterior propelling power. Thus the human soul is dependent upon motives for its forward movement. What hurled Paul along the highway of his life? What drove him toward mobbings, scourgings, prisons, and unto death itself? That chariot of the Greek god was hurled forward by the fiery steeds of the sun, but as for Paul, in his eager, passionate desire to serve gladiators, slaves, fugitives, prisoners, the word, "The love of Christ constraineth me," holds his secret. What led that Roman boy who had just heard the story of the Carpenter upon the Cross, that Roman boy who was a slave, and came in from the field to find that his young master had drowned, to his brave death of sacrifice? He simply asked for the place where his young master had gone down, and though they held him back, leaped into the black flood, felt around on the bottom of the lake, and at last found and brought up the body, yet died himself. Surely there was a motive back of this Roman boy's deed, and it proved to be in the sentence, "he that loseth his life shall save it."

Recall also that cripple in Switzerland, when the

army of the Austrians was crossing the mountain pass. A great love of country welled up in the heart of the little hunchback. So when the sentinels felt that all was safe, because the heavy snowfall had come, and they flung themselves down to sleep, the cripple, at midnight, when all was still, kept his window up, drew the blankets a little closer, and with his head out in the snow listened, straining to hear the slightest sound. It was his vigilance that detected the approach of the enemy. It was that cripple who wakened the sentinels, and the sentinels roused the soldiers, and the soldiers went up to the pass and held that narrow defile, and saved the valley. What miracles the love of country hath wrought! What a transformer love is! What impossible feats it has accomplished! Ten thousand beautiful philanthropies were born when Jesus said, "The angels do always behold the face of My Father." "Inasmuch as ye have done it unto one of the least of these My little ones, ye have done it unto Me." There is on a certain tropic tree a purple blossom, at the end of the bough. Travelers say that if you touch that crimson heart, you slay the glorious shrub. Not otherwise touch at your peril Christ, with His love of the poor and the weak, and the reforms, and the beautiful philanthropies perish also!

If there were no Christ, then the immortal hope perishes with Him. One December day, Harriet Martineau wrote her friend, saying: "For England the summer has gone, and for me the everlasting winter has set in." When James Mill gave up the Christ, he said "that the clouds had slowly closed in and choked all hope." Death had become only a leap into the dark, over a chasm, whose sharp rocks held an unknown power for mangling. The philosophers argued. The poets have hoped for a meeting place of the dead. The lovers have cried out for the beloved one. The parents have sobbed, "Is death a door into another room? Or a fall into a hole in the ground?" Then Jesus stood at the gate of the sepulchre. His message concerned the life immortal. What others talked about, He saw. His forehead grazed the stars. He looked over the top of the hill, named man's horizon, and saw afar off the sweet fields of living green in the land of pure delight. He plucked fear out of men's souls as the husbandman plucks the tare out of the wheat, as the physician plucks the foul growth out of the fair body, and restores it to full health. He taught men that dying was home-going; that heaven was the Father's house, and that nothing could ever injure God's children, either here or there, either before death or after death. The sweetest music that ever fell on the ears of humanity are the words, "In my Father's house are many mansions." "Let not your heart be troubled, neither let it be afraid." Not until men prefer fog bank to wheat harvests, the will o' the wisp to the guiding star; not until they prefer candles flickering into the socket, to the summer-making sun, will they prefer these tawdry little superstitions before that Divine Teacher, whose music is sphere-music, and whose voice is the melody of the world.

XII

THE UNEXPECTED VISITATIONS OF GOD

"Thou knewest not the time of thy visitation."—LUKE xix: 44.

FROM the Mount of Olives Jesus looked over upon Jerusalem, with its temple, its palaces, its streets, in the zenith of their splendour and the perfection of their beauty. He saw the people thronging the shops, buying and selling, marrying and given in marriage, all unconscious of the storm, big with calamity, hanging just above their heads. King Herod in his palace, the Chief Priest in his temple, saw no outer sign of the approaching retribution, and yet the time of visitation and penalty had fully come. There was a foul palace, where a king lived like a pig in a sty; there was a corrupt Temple, where "the Temple ring" rioted rather than feasted; there was a rotten court, a rotten camp, and a rotten people. Every crowded city during the fiery summer sends up foul gases and exhalations, that hold lightnings latent, but destructive. And Jerusalem, with its sensuality and cruelty, its greed and oppression, carried within itself the beginning and the end of penalty and retribution. Every nation holds at least one epoch that illustrates this principle of self-retribution. Witness France in 1789. Never had Louis been so firmly established upon his throne. The French language was universal, the French court was most brilliant, the foreign guards most faithful, and yet Marie Antoinette and Louis had no eyes to see the black cloud gathering above the palace. To the King and Queen the stroke of the revolution was a thunderbolt out of a blue sky, while for men of vision the tornado had been long overdue.

He who obeys the law of God finds the divine law resting upon his shoulders with the lightness of a gossamer thread, while he who disobeys God's law finds that law an iron fetter that weighs him down. Jesus saw revelry and frivolity in the streets below, and calamity impending from the heavens above. And He wept for the Temple that would soon be a waste and the city to become a desolation.

Wise men see that all divine visitations are natural, and not arbitrary and capricious. The term visitation means the coming of God to individuals, cities and nations. From the superficial viewpoint the divine approach is secret, unexpected and unprepared for. In reality, the visitations approach step by step, stage by stage, with the evenness of the approach of summer or winter. Doubtless this misapprehension springs out of a careless reading of the great events of history. Every nation has its own story of a flood, and every tradition represents the storm as coming suddenly, overtaking the people like a waterspout. While the men of Sodom were revelling and indulging in their orgies, the fire broke out, and under the impulse of a mighty wind the flames consumed the city in a single night. Belshazzar assembled a thousand lords for the great feast in his palace, when suddenly there was the handwriting on the wall. Secretly, the judgment, "Thou art weighed in the balances and art found wanting," was pronounced. Unexpectedly the gates of the city went down before the rush of the invading army, and when the sun rose the palace was in the hands of the besieging army, and Belshazzar and his lords went down under the retributions of an outraged people. When the atmosphere of a city is foul with poison, when mephitic gases threaten the springs of health and life, it must needs be that the lightning burn away the poison and make the atmosphere sweet and clean, that the harvest wind may blow over untainted fields. The coming of the electric bolt may be sudden, but the preparation thereof is slow, natural and ordered. By law, the dew distills. By law, the snowflakes form and fall. By law, the seasons come and go. By law, the clouds store their secret forces. By law, the thunderbolt is let fly along its appointed path. By law Belshazzar and Herod went toward their retribution and overthrow.

No judgment of God upon Sodom or Jerusalem, Paris or Peking is an arbitrary and wanton judgment. Every evil man, city and empire slowly prepares the explosives that by natural processes bring about their own retribution.

To the outer eye, when the giant tree goes down in the forest, it goes suddenly and unexpectedly, but to the close observer, the preparation for the fall covered months and years. Slowly the worm cuts its way to the heart of the tree; slowly the rain swells the tiny hole, the frost loosens, the heat enlarges the aperture; slowly the gases and acids begin to cut the fibre; little by little the decay goes toward the heart. Outwardly the bark is sound. To the boy's eyes, the great tree seems easily the king of the forest, and yet the heart is hollow, and the tree is a mere shell. One day there is a sound of the winds' going in the tree tops, and suddenly, the huge tree comes crashing down, and lo, it had a rotten heart! Thus the day came, when the armies of Titus were encamped round about Jerusalem. The walls fell, the Temple doors gave way, and not one stone was left upon another. But no temple can defend itself. No city gate can lift the weapon or be its own watchman. The Hebrew manhood had gone, and therefore the capital fell. The Hebrew soldier had lost his courage; the Jewish statesman had lost his justice; the priests and Levites had lost the ethical note. The people had become feeblings, manhood had decayed at the heart, and the nation was dead. Soon a handful of Roman soldiers laid waste the capital, and destroyed the whole country because the powers of resistance had broken down. Jesus read Jerusalem like an open book. Beholding the city that had no defenders, He wept, crying: "Oh, Jerusalem, Jerusalem, if thou hadst but known the day of thy visitation." Blind to the signals that were hanging from the battlements of heaven, deaf to the overtures of God, the people went toward ruin, and the uttermost of desolation.

To the practical man, these unexpected visitations of God are redemptive. There are four types of destiny, and to each of the four there comes the overture of God to a nobler and juster life. As the type of the man of affairs, living by reason, prudence and foresight, let us take Jacob, who has so largely shaped the character of the Hebrew people. In retrospect, he was the best equipped youth of his time. He was cautious, conservative, laying out his life on long plans, and safeguarding his interests against any possible peril. His older brother, Esau, under the law of the time, should have fallen heir to the estate and carried on the family name. But Esau was an Epicurean. A pleasure-lover, he lived for the body, with rich foods and wines, with soft raiment and brilliant equippage. For Esau, one hour of pleasure today was worth a dozen hours of possible safety tomorrow. Moreover, the impulsive youth, full of animal spirits, frivolous and wasting his substance with his riotous fellows, secretly despised the family name, and cared nothing for the title. Nothing can be baser than Esau's overture to Jacob, that he would surrender the right to represent the family and be the leader thereof, if Jacob would give to him the money for his orgies, that is represented by the words, "the mess of pottage." The stern and just man would say that it served Esau right. But in his unwillingness to wound his father's feelings, when the day came that the blind father was to hand over the leadership to his son, in the presence of the assembled servants Jacob played a trick upon the father, to the horror of the onlooking servants, whose excitement and protestation revealed to Isaac that something was wrong.

In such an era it was Esau, the hail-fellow-well met, impulsive, open-handed, convivial, free, generous, that had the heart of the people in his hand. The servants looked upon Jacob as hard-fisted and close, not knowing that there was better substance in the second brother for the building of a great family. And then God came to the deceiver, Jacob. A divine messenger knocked upon the door of conscience. The youth wakened to realise his sin. Jacob was strong, and Esau was weak. Jacob had skill, foresight and resource, and Esau was frivolous and idle. Jacob was an athlete who had taken advantage of his weaker brother. Shame struck him through and through. Fear overwhelmed Jacob. Conscience prodded him as with a sword's point. Ashamed, and full of grief, Jacob planned a worthy deed. Instead of claiming the right of family leadership, he determined to go away and leave his brother Esau in full possession. Instead of asking his portion of goods that belonged to him, he surrendered all his own goods to Esau, and went out to become the architect of his own fortune. It was as if the oldest son on an English estate should go into hiding that his younger brother, less resourceful, might fall heir to the castle and all the wide-lying acres. It was a splendid conception, nobly carried out. To repentance Jacob added restitution. Then he fled into the night, and started across the desert, hundreds of miles, toward a distant land where his uncle lived. But God did not meet the repentant sinner half way. He who in true sorrow, and after due restitution of his wrong, has turned toward God, finds that heaven has come a long way to meet him. Alone in the desert, with a stone for his pillow, and the night wind for his blanket, and the light of the firefly for a candle, with tears and sobs, Jacob cried out that though all things else had been taken away, mother, father, home and name he asked that God would not take away His presence. In his dream he saw that heaven was not far off, that a very short ladder sufficed to reach from his pillow of stone to the battlements of God. He saw the angels of memory taking his prayers and penitence up to God, and the angels of pity descending with messages of forgiveness.

And this practical man represents a modern type. Many of you have heard of God by the hearing of your ears. Well equipped and well educated, you have found God in the heavens above and the earth beneath. The ordering of events, and the upward movement of society have become witnesses to a Power that makes for righteousness. Suddenly, in some critical hour of your life, knowledge through the intellect, became certainty for the heart. A divine visitation came to you. It was like the coming of the morning, when the sun in his unrivaled splendour breaks over the earth, and the bats and things of the night retreat to their caves, to be seen no more. In the hour of vision every ignoble thought fled away forever from Jacob. In such an hour it were easier to doubt the sun than to doubt that God is, and that

He is flooding your soul with waves of light and love.

The child needs no argument for the grapes when it is plucking the purple clusters. The bee needs no proof of honey when it is sipping the clover sweets. Dante needs no philosophy of affection when he is resting upon Beatrice's love. The scholar needs no book of apologetics in the hour when God, the Great Physician, has approached with medicine to heal wounds, with pity to forgive sins, with love to redeem the life. No ingenious and gifted youth but has known one such golden hour of divine visitation. These are life's great moments. Oh! write them down forever upon the book of memory! To the mariner, carrying his ship, his cargo and passengers across the sea after days of fog and clouds, there comes a moment when the north wind cleaves a way through the mist. For one moment the sun shines out—but that moment, short as it is, is long enough for the captain to take his bearings and set his compass. The mists may shut down again, but the captain knows just where he is, and he sets his compass, knowing that he shall make the distant harbour and drop anchor in the desired harbour. And henceforth Jacob had his bearings! He set his moral timepiece by the divine Sun, and through that visitation of God, he became at length the prince and founder of the commonwealth of God.

This unexpected visitation of God sometimes works strange transformations upon men who have set their hearts upon things material. One of the richest trees in the Garden of Eden is the tree of property. God planted that tree, and fed its roots, and ripened clusters of abundance for those who looked to Him for daily bread. The love of property is as lawful and praiseworthy in the individual as is the love passion. Property is necessary for the State. Society does well to honour him whose industry, prudence and economy keeps his family from beggary, vice and shame. This love of property is one of the forces that hurls the chariot of the soul forward along life's highway. But what if a man who plants the tree of wealth should finally come to love the tree for its own sake? That is why the word for the miserable man is the word "miser." Having planted the tree in the world garden, when the clusters are ripe they are to be used for food. But what if the man who tends that tree should drop his spade and seize a club, and shout to the hungry children, "Stand off! Let no one touch these clusters! They are too precious to be eaten. I planted this tree! I ripened this fruit and food! What is mine is mine!" Meanwhile children weep and clusters rot!

Strange, this perversion! Passing strange this turning of the husbandman against himself! The eye was made for light, but he who misuses the eye will find the light become a torture. Conversation is pleasant to the ears, for the ear was made for hearing; but he who misuses his nerve force can reach a point where every sound is torture. God made property to ripen fruit—not for the next generation, but for the people of today. Strange that men can so misuse their gifts that they lose all the power to pluck the clusters for feeding the poor and weak. Such a man was Dives. God gave him rich harvests because there were orphans and poor people. The children's arms were spread wide to receive the fruit, but Dives turned his back on the little children and built huge barns instead of harvesting this treasure into children's hands. And then he said, "Soul, thou hast much goods laid up for many years." But what word is this, "Soul—thou hast corn!" Can a soul eat corn? Can the intellect and the memory consume wheat? Can the taste and the imagination drink oil and wine? Corn was made for the body. If Dives' body had enough corn, plainly the surplus was for the poor and the weak who had no bread. The children pleaded and the poor sobbed, and the beggar died in his rags and poverty. Meanwhile heaven was silent—that is as it were, silent. But all the time along the highway from heaven might have been seen an approaching figure—only this angel that comes is the angel of Justice. Suddenly the sword, red with insufferable wrath against selfishness, leaps from its scabbard.

Dives is dead—on earth they carry his body to his tomb under velvet plumes. But Dives' soul stands at the gate of the city of God. And lo, the angel with the flaming sword stands in the way, forbidding his passage. Dives' soul had no place in heaven. Dives lived for corn. Let him die as the corn dies. Retribution had come. The separation is here. There is a chasm digged between selfishness and love, between iniquity and integrity. There is a great gulf and abyss that stands between Dives' barns and God's palace of amethyst and silver, into which He has brought the orphans that Dives despised. Oh, that this generation had eyes to see and ears to hear. Look at the colossal fortunes, while the hundred thousand families that piled them up, live in hovels! Our modern Dives has done no stroke of work for twenty years. Meanwhile, the children sob, and heaven is silent. But be not deceived! Heaven is not mocked. Silence does not mean forgetfulness. There is a God in the sky. Human judgments will be reversed. What if the last poor workman in yonder rude hut, who has toiled on faithfully, without bitterness or hate or weapon, shall be first before God, while Dives stands forth the last call! Alas for Dives, that takes up sobs in the hour when he lifts up his voice, "If I had but known! Oh, if I had but known the day of God's visitation!" while he weeps over the ruined City of Mansoul.

Strange visitations come to the men who represent lawless ambition. The historic representative of this type is Saul, the most gifted man of his day. In his youth his father's wealth gave him leisure to study in the school of Gamaliel and to travel in foreign lands. Ambitious, he set his heart on promotion, and determined to get on. The pathway to glory was through the Sanhedrim. That group of men included in themselves control of the lands, the offices, the gold, and the power of the country. Unfortunately for young Saul, no man could belong to the Sanhedrim who was not old and mature. That law was inflexible and never varied. Desperate, young Saul determined to break into that magic circle. Fortunately for his lawless ambition, the Sanhedrim fronted a crisis. This new faith of Christ was spreading among the people. An old member of the Sanhedrim, Gamaliel, stood up and argued, "If it be of God we cannot fight it, and if it be not of God it will come to naught. Let us do nothing." Other members had the spirit which centuries later possessed Torquemada and the Inquisition, but because they were old they were timid, and did not dare fling themselves against the new faith. Their Inquisition needed youth, dash, ignorance and lawless ambition, and they made overtures to young Saul. Shrewd, ambitious, selfish, Saul organised persecution, yet himself stood in the background. Just as today men who have organised combinations to destroy the poor and prepared cunning schemes to evade the laws, have put clerks and puppets forward upon whom the state will execute its judicial penalties, so in that far-off era Saul stood off and kept the garments of his puppets who stoned Stephen to death. But "when ambition soars too near the sun the heat melts away the golden wings." Saul found that blood was valuable to wash ambition's hands.

And now that Saul has won the approval of the leaders of the Sanhedrim, and the prize is within his reach, he looks for more cities to conquer, and more disciples to persecute, and starts toward Damascus. It was a long journey, and the way was solitary. Solitude is terrible for a man with a guilty deed upon his conscience, and blood upon his hands! Nothing can be more awful than for some Macbeth to be alone at night, while God's stars blaze at him, and keep blazing. Oh, these stars that would not let Saul sleep! The whole sky at night became a divine forehead, out of which blaze these two stars, always two and two! What Saul feared was the God of justice. There was a God of justice behind the stars. This sun, too, at high noon, with light insufferable, scorched his soul. Conscience became unendurable. Saul now saw Stephen's face shining as he lay dying, with the splendour of heaven upon his face. In an agony of remorse he cried aloud. By the way of sin he had gone toward the throne of justice, only to find it was a throne of mercy. The divine visitation had come. Reason that had whispered warnings began to thunder. The praise of men in the Sanhedrim seemed as nothing in the face of the condemnation of God. In an agony of remorse he cried out unto God, and fled into the sands of Arabia, where he remained for three years. He put distance between that Sanhedrim, with its temptations to lawless ambition, and himself. He obeyed the divine visitation. He listened to the warnings that fell from the battlements of heaven. What changed Saul the Inquisitor, to Paul, the hero and martyr? Why, that visitation of God to a youth of unbridled ambition, melting him into obedience, self-surrender, and loyalty to God. If Saul had not known the day of God's visitation, the disaster would have been one of the greatest moral disasters in the annals of time.

To all men come these overtures divine. Wonderful these moments when truth glows in the soul like flame in the coal. In hours when the reason is struck through and through with light, men are not far from the kingdom of God. Are not luminous hours, hours of destiny? They are sometimes as brief as the strategic moment that comes to the astronomer watching an eclipse. Only for a moment is shadow there, and then the eclipse passes, so the scientist must be ready for that moment. If all things are ready, the astronomer carries away upon his plate the record of the movement of sun and planet, and human culture is enriched by the new knowledge. But if the astronomer is careless and sleeps during that precious moment, then the great opportunity is lost, and once lost is lost forever. Thus when these luminous moods come to man the one duty is instant action, immediate decision, and irrevocable pledges. The old man, grown callous and hard, may be tempted to reject these moods, counting them mere sentimentalism, and despising them as emotional. A dead soul is like yonder dead moon. What if you could sit down and talk with the spirit of that dead world as you talk with a familiar friend? Suppose the moon should say, "Once I believed in the procession of the seasons. Once I waited for the blowing of the south wind, the arbutus blossom, the tender grass and the flaming orchards. Once I spread my boughs for the birds and sheltered the beasts against the storm. But that is all gone. Now I am practical. I have gotten down to hard pan. I believe in solid rock. No more perfumed sentiments for me. No more ideals and aspirations." Alas! for the dead soul that has lost its ideals, given up its dreams and reveries, its secret prayers and hidden hopes. The wise man will cherish these noble moods. He will nurture these moments big with character and destiny! So that is what it is to be a practical man!

XIII

NO CULTURE WITHOUT STUDY, NO CHARACTER WITHOUT WORSHIP

"And as his custom was, he went into the synagogue on the sabbath day."—LUKE iv: 16.

THERE are eighteen silent years in the life of Jesus. These years, like the throne of God, are surrounded with clouds and mystery. For one brief moment, when He was about twelve years of age, the curtains parted, and we see the face of an eager boy, standing in the Temple, on the Sabbath Day, both asking and answering questions. But the curtain falls again and when, eighteen years later, we catch another glimpse of the young Carpenter, He is standing in the Temple, on the Sabbath, with the sacred roll in His hand. What influences entered into those plastic years of the greatest and most beautiful figure in history, we do not know! Did He ever enter the class room of some noble teacher, as Paul sat at the feet of Gamaliel? As Aristotle listened to Plato? There were several Greek cities founded by Alexander upon the shores of Lake Galilee; did Jesus meet in one of those towns the Greek merchants who visited Him later in Jerusalem? And did they ever show Him their books of Homer and Hesiod, and Herodotus? To the north, a day's journey, was that financial centre, Damascus.

What were Jesus' thoughts when He stood in their market place? Where the commerce of four nations met and mingled. To the west of Nazareth, within one brisk morning's walk, were the high cliffs from which Jesus looked down upon the Mediterranean, white with the sails of ships, carrying wheat to Rome. Many powerful influences united to emancipate Jesus from the limitations of race, class, colour, and sex. He was the first human being that loved all races, pitied all, helped all. Other influences must have done something to make Him a teacher, not of the Hebrew race, but of the human race. We are certain that the one overmastering influence in His growing life was the influence of His invariable custom of worship in the synagogue on the Sabbath. Within sacred walls He read and re-read and received into His memory, the great mother ideas of right and wrong, and duty, as set forth in the laws of Moses. Again and again He pondered the story of the national heroes, Abraham, and Joseph, Saul and Daniel, of the Judges, Samuel and Eli and Gideon; of the poets, Job, and David, with the visions of Isaiah. Oft, He brooded over the social ideals of Amos and Malachi. Oft in solitude He dreamed His dreams of a new social order and a golden age. Often, too, in the night, under the stars, alone while other men slept, He saw the rift in the sky, and heard the voices falling, and in an ecstacy of joy and tears left far below the little house and the old workshop, and walked the streets of the unseen and beautiful City of God.

Now the very genius of Jesus' character and the

whole ordering of His life are revealed in the fact that His custom of worship on the Sabbath was an example that He made binding upon His disciples. Beyond any other religious Teacher whatsoever, Jesus insisted upon the necessity and the duty of worship, for His disciples.

That which was vital in His own religious experience was made obligatory for His disciples. "Whatever is best and necessary for the children of genius should be made a duty and a habit of lesser men," wrote a philosopher. Jesus had no artificial habits. Whatever He did grew out of the nature of things. By example and by teaching He taught the custom of worship. "What," asks James Martineau, "had Jesus not risen above that? Could the dull preachings and the drawling prayers say anything to Him? What charm could He longer feel, in these childish Sabbath usages, the decent dress, the restful hours, the flowing together of families, and walking to the house of God in their company. Did not He, above all, live in a constant air of divine communion, and mingle with the eternity where all is consecrated alike Himself a better sanctuary than He could ever find? Yet, He went at Nazareth, where He had been brought up, He went, as His custom was, into the synagogue on the Sabbath Day." By Christ's example and teaching He made the Church and its aisles, crowded with young and old, stand by day and night, a witness to the world of invisible and heavenly things.

Universal experience reinforces Jesus' insistence upon regular and systematic worship in church on

Sunday. In his study of the Scholar, Emerson found in habit the greatest friend of intellectual culture. Religion is life, God's life, in man's soul. But life develops under rules, through laws. Dead things accumulate, and increase by chance; there is no hit and miss in the growth of living things. The soil is dead, and accumulates falling leaves, boughs, star dusts, just as coral reefs are accumulations of dead cells. Living things, sheaves, roots, birds, babes,—grow. Man's body grows by obeying the laws of food, sleep and exercise. Man's intellect grows by reading, reflection, conversation and travel. Man's culture grows through a little hard study every day. By practice the orator or actor wins a rich resonance for his voice. Every singer knows the peril through flabbiness that follows the neglect of the vocal cords. "How did you achieve your supremacy?" asked an actor of Wendell Phillips; and the instant answer of the orator was: "By getting a thousand nights back of me." Turner understood. Talking to his pupils he said: "Draw! draw! Paint, paint, and still paint, and then tear up your work and begin another canvas." Once, during an important banquet in Paris, Rodin was seen to take from his pocket a bit of bronze. Turning it over and over, he soaked his mind in its beauty. The greatest sculptor of modern times was a learner up to the last hour of his life. Now if the artist learns to paint by painting; if orators learn to speak by speaking; if authors learn to write by writing, then disciples must learn to pray and pity, and love and serve, by praying, and loving, and serving. Genius is the capacity for infinite details and terrible toiling. From His earliest waking moment to the last minute of conscious life, Jesus practiced the presence of God, and by practice increased daily in favour with God. He went about doing good, and practiced service. The very genius of His life and education is in the words, "And as His custom was, He went into the synagogue on the Sabbath Day." It seems, therefore, that when the long-awaited moment arrived, when He was to begin His ministry, that He went naturally into the synagogue on the Sabbath, and with a sacred roll in His hand stood up and announced that the moment for which the whole world had long waited had come. In an act of worship, He announced His programme for the kingdom of God and the Golden Age.

Thoughtless people often associate rule, habit, and system with mediocrity, and think of genius in terms of moods, occasional spurts, and instance the spasmodic Burns, and Byron. But the view is as silly as it is mistaken. There never lived a man of undoubted genius who did not control his life by habit and system. Michael Angelo, architect, sculptor, painter, poet, had the ability of twenty talented men, but he controlled his genius by habit, just as Watt and Stephenson controlled the steam engine within chambers of steel. Bacon and Isaac Newton arose at daybreak to begin work at the stroke of the clock. Ability is like the wild steed of the prairie, it must be caught, harnessed, and drilled to carry man's burden. The greater the gift, the more rigidly the control by rule. Witness

Kant, author of the *Critique of Pure Reason,* who divided his work and scarcely varied his plan five minutes a day through forty years. But this is Nature's method. The arbutus is always sweet—the perfume is mixed each spring, to an unchanging formula. The flavour of the strawberry is wrought out by rule.

Summer is systematic, and the ripeness of the harvest is the outer exhibition of an inner obedience to law. Spontaneity? A handful of violets plucked at dawn, and all dripping with dew, are not fresher than the songs of King David, who exclaimed, "Morning, and noon, and night do I pray." Wordsworth's reference to the loveliness of his *Ode to the Skylark* shows that he never neglected his gift, bestowed by God and his fathers, but without reference to his feelings he began work at seven o'clock each day. In early spring days, when the whole South is a brilliant flower garden, when every wind is loaded with perfume, the scientist explains the loveliness and the freshness of the scene by obedience to laws, to a sun that is never a moment late in its shining, to the tides that ebb and flow in accordance with rule, to the berries, the grains, the cotton, and the wool that are always fashioned in accordance with the strictest formulæ, scrupulously obeyed. Imagine trying to live in a world of irregularity, hit and miss, and chance! What if you wakened to find that if heat made the coffee hot one morning, the flame froze the water the next; what if cane sugar being sweet last summer, were acid this year? What if the sunbeams that warmed in the morning, froze everything in the afternoon? What if one babe were born with two feet, and two eyes, and the next babe with three feet and one eye? In a world of moods, of hit and miss, what is called spontaneous decisions, man would go crazy, art would be impossible, tools an idle dream, and the very word science a figment of the imagination. Thank God, we are in a world where the husbandman, the scientist, the artist and the Christian are controlled by laws, that are invariable. The greatness of a man is determined by the number of the laws he learns and obeys. For laws are not weights,—but wings; they are not fetters, they are open doors. And Jesus controlled His gifts by law, lived by rule, made His piety systematic, and His kindness was a controlled service, and His worship of God as invariable as the rise of the sun.

Of late the American people have been startled by what is called a crime wave. Our jurists explain the steady, regular increase in lawlessness by the fact that a generation has now come to maturity that had little or no moral instruction whatsoever. Twenty years ago the parents of our country gave up the Sunday School and church for their children, and transferred the emphasis upon education to the intellect for five days of the week. Truant officers were appointed in the cities to see that all children were in school, daily between nine o'clock and three. Parents forced their children to give up truancy, and made them study five hours a day. Fathers realised that there was no place in business for boys that know nothing of arithmetic, reading, geography, history, and their allied subjects. Force, therefore, was invoked by both the state and the parent. Today, even for boys who intend to drop out of school at fifteen, there are eight years of constant drill and study.

But when it comes to the Ten Commandments, the general principles of obedience to the laws of our country, of the home and business, parents refuse to make their children master the principles of morals.

Witness these jails of ours, stuffed with children! Witness the three murders within a little distance of this old church! Witness a little town of twenty-five thousand, that has had seven murders in one year! The million young people arrested for stealing last year, may soon be two million! But the Ten Commandments are not denominational, any more than the multiplication table is denominational. There is nothing sectarian about the laws of our state or our country. And the laws of the Christian religion are natural laws, that are as binding upon Jews, Catholics, Mohammedans, Buddhists, followers of Confucius, as are the laws of steam, electricity, or chemistry. Several sects, for reasons of self and ambition, oppose teaching in the public school the moral principles that Webster once said are a part of "the common law of our land." To prepare our children for business we invoke the truant officer, who uses threats and arrest to compel children to attend school, and acquire knowledge necessary for self-support. Strange that millions of parents refuse to compel their children to study the fundamental moral principles that are vital to their success in life. Little wonder that men associate race hatreds, wars, poverty, and the collapse of civilisation abroad with the passing of Sunday and moral education. Less wonder is it that men are beginning to ask whether the Sunday has gone for a republic that was based by our fathers upon intellectual and moral illiteracy, with full training as to the great facts of human life.

Many years have passed since Robert Collyer began his ministry in the Church of the Messiah by telling his people that a generation before, in the Unity Church of Chicago, he had told his hearers to go into the park, forest, or out upon the lake, on Sunday, if they thought that they could worship God to better purpose there than within the walls of a church. And how he had found later, through experience, that men who did not worship God at one time and at one place, with other families, soon ceased to worship God at all, and starved to death their religious faculty. And that when men refused to bow their knees before God, they stopped bowing the mind and the heart. And for that reason Robert Collyer insisted that Jesus was right, and that the custom of worship is absolutely necessary to any growth for the spirit of man. Thoreau tried to be a hermit in a little log cabin. He isolated himself for study, but found that his mind began to atrophy, being starved for companionship. Every teacher knows that contact for pupils with other minds and with the teacher, is a stimulant to personal culture.

Centuries ago the monks tried by isolation and the cell or the desert to make the most of the soul, by unceasing prayer, reflection, and denial of the body and its appetites, with the inevitable result—they grew selfish, vain, harsh, narrow, and discontented. What they needed was contact with their fellows while they went about doing good. The reflex influence of selfish club life, also, illustrates the same peril. Witness the decline of hospitality! What multitudes of mature people stand forth isolated, with but a little handful of friends left! They have forgotten how to keep their friendships in repair. When Darwin's health broke, and his physicians insisted upon his giving up scientific study, the scientist turned toward the drama and music, only to discover that after forty years of neglect neither comedy nor tragedy, nor opera meant anything to him! He had starved to death those faculties until they had become atrophied through neglect. It seems, therefore, that when Jesus went to the synagogue on the Sabbath Day, and with His friends fulfilled the duties of worship, He had behind Him all the sanctions of the intellect, with its culture, all that is best in the growth of the faculties artistic, musical, literary and scientific.

It is a sad reflection upon the superficiality of the modern intellect, with its frivolity, and incapacity for fundamental thinking, that men are found, who say they need Sunday for recreation, physical exercise, and that they are too tired to adopt for themselves Jesus' method of self-culture. This is equivalent to a confession by some men that they are not equal intellectually to the support of a family, and at the same time do their part to defend and use aright the Sunday as the only college day, library day, home day, for the working people and for foreigners, who need instruction in morals, and American culture. Therefore, by their example, they steadily break down the Sunday, undermine the Christian religion, and are what Webster called "unconfessed enemies of the Republic." They expect ministers, teachers, and a few men of extraordinary ability, to educate in morals the children and youth of the land, while they sponge upon the nation and its resources. Still others say they can get more out of the newspapers in the early Sunday morning hours than they can out of a church, or out of the sermon, preached by indifferent thinkers. But Jesus did not enter the synagogue on the Sabbath because the preacher was His superior, or because the sermon contained more wisdom than He could find in certain books. Jesus entered the synagogue for worship, prayer, friendship, reflection, and that He might meet and help His fellow-men, in a great moment when all souls were warm and plastic and struck through and through with light. His mere example refreshed His neighbours, rebuked their folly, inspired their loyalty, freshened their ideals. How shall the fifty millions of native Americans assimilate perhaps sixty-two millions of foreigners? Is there any better way than by turning one day out of every seven into a college and library day for the soul, when all adults bring to the conduct and character of thirty million children and youth the great divine principles of duty, and destiny, of love and obedience to God, and to country, and to God's dear Son, the great principles of Christian conduct and character. Could such a consummation be brought about, despite the alien radicals who fear nothing so much as the increase of the Christian spirit, this land could be made, within five years, to be a kind of new Eden, a paradise, without hate, poverty, moral illiteracy or crime.

Not less striking was Jesus' insistence that true worship is not solitary, but social. When flint and steel come together, something leaps forth that was not in either. Botanists know that what the individual cell cannot do, many cells easily accomplish. Just because innumerable leaves work together, they slowly build the forest tree. Because millions of vital cells unite, they build the human body with its strength and beauty. The family cannot exist until two unite their affection. Defoe tells us that everything started for Robinson Crusoe when the man Friday arrived, for two meant the beginning of a society. Every orator knows that when the audience is scattered, the argument moves slowly, but when the room is crowded and shoulders touch, the sacred spark leaps from heart to heart and soon all take flame. In the success of great revivals and political meetings a large part is played by physical and mental contact of its assembled thousands. The probabilities are that certain invisible and vital elements in each individual stream forth into the common air, and create a new atmosphere that not only becomes warm, summery and electric, but which is also charged with unseen and almost omnipotent forces.

In the new atmosphere surrounding the multitude made up of poor and rich, wise and ignorant, young and old, misunderstandings evaporate, hatreds dissolve, and enmities disappear. That is why a class church is treason to Jesus, who loved society. All hunters know that, left alone, the lighted match goes out, therefore the hunter first brings together many twigs and boughs, of various sizes and lengths, and then strikes the match, knowing that the flame will pass from bough to bough, until the whole becomes a mass of coal. And this was Jesus' method of unifying the classes, and filling up the gulf between Dives and Lazarus. The Gospel is the great unifier of the races. The Church is a family of which all the classes are members; it is a school in which all men are pupils; the Church is a hospital, in which all find healing and medicine, and this custom of worship in God's presence on the Sabbath Day, when all classes come together to sing and pray, and resolve, all being in the spirit of love and good will, represents Christ's plan for solving all economic and industrial problems. Today, if all rich men and poor would come together as brothers, to swear fidelity to the same Master, to breathe their common prayers unto a common Father, and to realise that the burdens of one are the burdens of all, to remember that the Church is Christ's League of Pity, that its members make up His "Beloved Society," and that whoever injures his brother has been guilty of treason toward the disciple band, that "each is for all, and all for each," all hate and strife would evaporate, poverty and crime would disappear, and the world would enter upon an era of prosperity and peace. Men have tried many expedients, many laws, many weapons, but some day they will try Jesus' plan, and then the discordant, warring classes will find that the paths of worship are paths that lead to social peace, brotherhood and prosperity.

XIV

WHAT IF THIS YEAR BE THE LAST!

"Thus saith the Lord; . . . this year thou shalt die."—JER. xxviii: 16.

IN view of his few brief years, man has the endowment of a god, the arena of an insect. The sand fly is born at daylight, dies at dark, but its life is long—for a sand fly. Man lives through seventy years, but these years are all too short for a being made in God's image. The vast endowments of the soul; its mastery over the forces of land and sea and sky; its unfulfilled places, all assume an existence, not of seventy years, but of seventy times seventy years. The average man spends his entire career in mastering one art, one profession, one industry, while all the other realms must be postponed to another career. Only now and then is there a Leonardo, or a Michael Angelo, who masters architecture, sculpture, painting, music, civil engineering and all in one life. Biography illustrates the brevity of our career. Our country has one inventor with two thousand patents to his credit, but he has spent seventy-two years on the electric light, the phonograph and the battery. In the world of literature, Coleridge was unique, but dying, he left one hundred manuscripts carefully outlined and big with promise, but not one of them complete. Shaftesbury was the leader of his generation in philanthropy, who worked for coal miners, chimney sweeps, orphans and castaways; but dying, Shaftesbury said that he had just started his reforms.

Coming to the end the falling statesman, the dying mother, the gifted boy, all exclaim, "Too short! Too short!" Moses felt the bitterness of life's brevity, and expressed that feeling by saying that his little life was like a falling leaf, a fading flower, a dissolving cloud, the summer's brook, the night watch between two days of battle, the tale told around the evening's fire, but forgotten when the morning comes. David, the poet king, also rebelled against life's brevity; his life was like the flight of a bird, the speed of an arrow, the stay of a postman, the glimpse of a passing ship. The wise king felt it; his life was like the flight of the eagle, that left no more mark upon the air, like the keel of a ship that leaves no mark upon the face of the water. Man is the weaver, the days are flying shuttles, the earth furnishes the framework, slowly the purple cloth is woven, but suddenly an enemy comes, to break the loom, and rend away the cloth, and ruin the weaver's house. Oh, this beautiful world! How eagerly men plan for many years packed with achievements! Looking out upon the stars, walking under the tranquil sky, beholding the beauty of the summer, singing the harvest song midst shock and sheaves, exulting midst the majesty and beauty of the winter—what lover of his fellow-men but wishes to stay in this beautiful world at least a thousand years? Then comes the warning as to life's brevity, "Man's days are as sparks falling upon a river."

Consider the contrast between material achievements that abide, and the invisible life of the soul that dissolves like a cloud filled with golden light. Go into the museum; lo, the bird tracks are fixed in sandstone, that received their impression ages ago. Enter old Warwick Castle. Here are dented helmets, broken shields, nicked swords, used by King Alfred's men, lo! all the knights are dust! Study the Egyptian room at the Metropolitan Museum of Art, and you behold the mummies yellow, dry, falling before the touch of a finger; but there, too, are the shrivelled seeds of wheat, that ripened three thousand years ago. Sown on good soil that grain will swell, germinate, put forth tall stalks, grow green and gold in the sun, and being sown again, with the process repeated for fifteen summers, lo, there is bread for the fifteen hundred millions of the children of men. Study the stump of the redwood tree whose seed was dropped into the soil twenty-five centuries ago, and the scientist finds some rings that represent years of heavy rain, and other narrow rings that represent years of drought. Needle and leaf were monument builders that left a permanent memorial behind them in the Mariposa groves of California. Strangely moved, the worker turns from the seeming permanency of things in wood and stone, and notes the fleeting, transient element in the noblest lives. The career of parent, patriot and teacher is like unto the shadow that falls upon the wheatfield when a cloud passes between the sun and the earth. The influence of the singer, the artist and the orator seems as fragile and evanescent as the landscapes etched by the angel of the frost upon the window in January. There is a bloom upon the cheek of the peach and the plum that is destroyed by one touch of the hand; and thus the work of many a hero sometimes seems to be as fleeting and perishable as that delicate flush upon the fruit. But man longs to be remembered. He wishes to build, not in ice, that dissolves, but in granite, that abides. Then comes the warning: "Thy days are like the foam upon the crest of the wave, iridescent for a moment, then broken and dissolved forever." Verily the time is short! Therefore, "what thou doest, do quickly!"

Now it was the sense of the shortness of His career that strained the Saviour of men to the most intense activity. History contains the record of no life that was so fruitful as his career that was packed with good deeds. Beginning His work at thirty years of age, Jesus toiled under an overhanging cloud that was not black with impending gloom but bright with approaching glory. He tells us plainly that He did not know what the future held in store as to the time or the manner of His death. In view of His open break with the State and the Church He felt His end could not be far off. Under the pressure, therefore, of the thought that His time was short, His mind fairly effulged with great thoughts. His days were packed with memorable deeds.

He was not content with opening the furrow

and sowing a few handfuls of grain—whoever tries to write the life of Christ will discover that all His days are like tropic fields, where the flowers and the rich herbs grow up so thick and luxuriant that they choke the wagon wheels. Every morning He wakened to unexampled ardour, and ceaseless activity. His genius struck off brilliant parables as sparks fly from the blacksmith's hammer, or as stars leap into being under the stroke of God's omnipotence. His so-called miracles were benefactions for the poor. Upon a single day He fed the hungry, opened fountains to lost pilgrims, lighted many a torch for the dark night in which the pilgrim floundered. Often, when every man went to his own house, it is said, with strange pathos, that Jesus went into the mountain, there to prepare His soul for new instruction and richer deeds of kindness when another day had come. What motive impelled Jesus to this intense activity? The bow flings an arrow toward its mark, and the Lord and Master of us all tells us plainly that the night cometh, that His time is short, that when the morrow's morrow doth come He must give His account of the work He had done. Fearing for the Master's life through our zeal Jesus' disciples led Him to a boat and put out upon the Lake of Galilee, that He might find sleep and restoration.

Another reaction from the sense of life's brevity is the spirit of unity, order and movement it gives to the advancing days. The danger of life is aimlessness. Soul drifting means the rapids and the precipice, and finally the fatal plunge. Every traveler who plans a visit to some foreign land lays out his program, and marks out a definite plan. What if some youth should go to the ticket office at the central station, and say, "Give me a ticket." And when the agent answered, "To what city? Chicago? Los Angeles? London?" And what if the youth should answer, "Oh, it makes no difference—I just want to go somewhere." Is not that an illustration of the way multitudes drift aimlessly from day to day and from year to year? Having no realisation of the brevity of life, or the importance of each week, their one aim is to kill time. These idling social parasites are saying, "How shall we kill January and February? In Havana? In Pasadena? In Egypt?" And in the spring they say, "Well, I suppose we must decide what we must do! What a bore it is to determine whether we shall go to the mountains or to the seashore." At the end of each day they wonder how they can kill the evening, as if time stuff was not the basis of greatness! As if all influence was not compacted hours! As if a great career was something other than days that march in solid columns toward a determined goal!

It is purpose that turns a mob into a regiment. It is a thought and motive that organises sounds into songs. It is a blue print that makes aimless bricks come together in a library or gallery. What biting sarcasm is in Dante's portrait of the soul drifters! Concerning that rich and pampered Florentine Prince and Princess, Dante said, "These are they who eat and drink and wear clothes—but no more. Therefore were they plunged into boiling mud." What the poet means is that these triflers, these industrial paupers, these epicureans, these pleasure mongers, were of fiery mud here, and beyond will again become boiling mud. No general waging a successful campaign waits and drifts. Rather, does he organise his regiments and make them march toward a goal. A plan by some Goethals stands behind every spadeful of dirt, and moves toward a goal, called a Panama waterway to the Pacific. The measure of this year's work will be the spirit of unity and purpose that makes the life march as one solid column of days, toward a far-off goal. In the interest, therefore, of prosperity, influence and increasing character, let every youth invoke the motive of life's brevity and the sense that, if art is long, the time is short and the emergency immediate.

Another impression gained from the survey of Jesus' life is His anticipation of the hour of home-going, when He should return to that imperial palace from whence He came, and give a report to His Father of the work He had accomplished upon the far flung battle frontier. Over and over again He talks of the coming revealing day when man shall come home after his fierce conflict with sin upon this far-off battlefield. Then shall all the good and great assemble to give Him greeting and tumultuous welcome. What a scene is that which Jesus opened up in His description of the Great Assize and the hour when honours and awards were distributed. He uttered no silly twaddle about doing work for work's sake, and being good for the sake of mere goodness, for all that was a mere matter of fact to be assumed by every man with an ounce of intellect.

But He talked openly about the great day of awards, and used imagery a thousand times more striking than that scene when the French Government distributes its prizes to the students and competitors in painting, music, poetry and dramatic literature. With powerful hand He draws back the curtains and shows us His Father upon the throne surrounded by all heroic souls out of all ages and climes, an assembly of the good and great. One by one the names are called out just as a harper strikes note after note. For one moment the individual disciple is to be the centre of the scene, upon whom all eyes are focussed. One by one those whom the man has blessed or cursed will rise, and their testimony be given. Every evil deed shall report itself at that hour. Every deflection from honour, every wicked evasion, every refusal of the great conviction, every hidden lie and theft and every evil influence shall be there. Men shall be seen, not as they think themselves to be, not as their friends suppose, but as they really are! Some of the obscure ones of the earth, who have been true to the high ideals, shall be lifted to thrones of influence! And some who have been first shall be last, as they are stripped of earthly honours, and in the presence of revered fathers and noble mothers shall shrink away, because they have no place among those who are true and faithful. And the verdict is "Of him will I be ashamed in the presence of My Father and His angels."

Christ's picture of the Last Judgment is the most highly wrought thing in literature. What man can read it without the anticipation of that great day of reward and penalty? What an appeal to self-respect! What a quickening of pride of blood and family! What an uprising of indignation against every influence that is evil! Oh, all yet young hearts, keep ever before you the outlook of that great day. As young scholars look forward to the day of testing before the noble teacher; as young soldiers anticipate the hour when they shall make a report to their brave general; live ever as in the Great Taskmaster's eye. Prepare your souls that you may not enter into unknown, unwelcomed, dishonoured, but rather awaited for by a great company, who come out to meet and greet you, and with trumpets and banners bring you in to be greeted by the heroes of the great convictions.

Because the time is short, in laying out his plans for the best possible use of his life, the prudent man will relate himself distinctly to those movements that make for human betterment. During these troubled and tumultuous days men carry heavy hearts. A million or more in India and China—our consuls say—starve to death every year. The men and women engaged in the relief work in the Near East and Europe say that several million children must be given at least half a loaf every day if they are to grow good bodies. Not one of you, surely, can go into your house, and pull down the curtains and feast, unless you first stuff wax in your ears to keep from being disturbed by the bitter cry of these children. If some are freezing in the snow outside, for those inside the winter's fire turns into ashes. Men who love their fellows must share their burdens. The race is become one. Every citizen must put away his selfish interests, and his racial prejudices, and become a citizen of the world. Not less important is it, for each man to reflect that if this year should be his last that he must make provision for his family, and safeguard their future. Just as captains when the barometer falls, even though the sky is perfectly clear, prepare for the rush and thunder of the inevitable cyclone; just as householders, upon the approach of winter, lay up a store of wood and coal against the bitter frost, so good men have their duties in founding the family that doubles their happiness. No man has a right to bring children into the world, without making provision against hunger and cold, in the event of their being orphaned. Every sentiment of honour rebukes parents who spend as much as they earn and who drift, thinking that society will lift the shield of protection above those for whom the father was thoughtless and indifferent. Some of the darkest tragedies ever known have come from the unexpected death of a careless husband. Who has not known at heart one noble woman of posittion, culture and friendship, left in the hour of her husband's death, exposed to the fury of life's storm; left to move now from a home among her friends to some tenement region, and then to sell her furniture, piece by piece, until at last she is in a garret, cold and cheerless? How wonderful that such an one in that dark hour maintains a beautiful faith and a forelook of better things to come, keeping ever the note of distinction in her heart! When the tragedy is complete, what indignant emotions arise in the hearts of the friends of that careless husband and father who was so indifferent to the future! Considerations of prudence and honour should lead every citizen to reflect that his year may be his last year. All his plans should be wise plans, representing thrift, economy and safety for those who dwell within the golden circle of his home.

Because this new year may be his last year, many a man will do well to linger in memory upon the years that are past. It is often said that the past is irreparable; that once the water has gone over the dam it cannot be recovered; that the evil that men do lives after them, and that yesterdays hold a record that can never be changed. More than forty years ago, out in a Western city, upon the edge of an Indian reservation that was about to be thrown open to settlers, there stood a covered wagon of an immigrant, in which were an old man and his nephew. Hard by was a farmer's home, with whom the two immigrants boarded, and had their daily meals. One night the uncle and his nephew disagreed, and, packing his satchel, the youth bade good-by to his uncle and to the farmer's family and started back to his old home. The next morning that farmer rushed to a neighbour's house to say that this uncle had been killed, plainly by his nephew and that five thousand dollars that the uncle had upon his person, with which to buy the new farm, had been stolen. Soon the officers of the law overtook that nephew, brought him back to the scene of the crime, tried and executed the boy. Shortly after, the farmer sold his farm and moved to another State and the memory of the crime passed out of men's minds.

Thirty years came and went again. One day an aged man reappeared at the old farm, that he had sold so many years before. He returned to say that the nephew was innocent—that he himself had slain that boy's uncle, and stolen the five thousand dollars; that in another State he had prospered, but that the load had become too heavy to carry; that he hungered for penalty. Before the judge he lifted up his hand and said, "I am a perjurer, I am a thief, I am a murderer," and then, within a few weeks, in the little jail, he fell upon death. This law of retribution works remorselessly. Every wicked man must make confession and restitution here or yonder. Last spring a great business man passed in review a career somewhat dramatic of a notorious character. He said, "That man has sold his soul unto the devil. Beginning in a good home, with everything in favour of an honest life, he has at last gone down, step by step, until he has become a moral idiot. Evil has at last become his good." And then he told the story of the loss of a man's soul; how he had betrayed confidence and been charged with the misuse of trust funds; how he had reappeared in a Western State and, once again under suspicion, was saved by a fire that burned all documents. Then came another removal to a distant State, with other deflections from the laws of honour in the college, until he had to leave that California town within twenty-four hours. At last, touching the bottom, he robbed a mission of its trust funds and clothed his family and paid the expense for his own passions with what had been given by the poor for the endowment of their own work and ended with a "plant" against a bookkeeper, to conceal his own sins. "In a moral universe can that man conceal a horde accumulated by theft? Will not the day come when he will hear sounding through the air, 'Thou whited sepulchre!' and the thunderbolt of an outraged God strike him dead with a perjury upon his mildewed lips! Can a wicked man prosper by wickedness? When he has not one single morsel of food or thread of raiment that other hands did not create? Wisdom refuses to believe it." But that verdict of this man of large experience is based on a partial outlook. Many a wicked man has prospered in this life and to the end. For the complete epic there must be added the dramatic chapter that comes through "The Life Beyond." Sometime, somewhere, that man will have to lift his hand, and in the presence of the good and the great, and of a just God, and cry out, "Thief!" "Perjurer!" "Liar!" "Unclean! Unclean!" "Some men's sins go beforehand unto judgment, and some men's sins follow after." But there may be recovery, through the fires of full confession and restitution, that consume the crime, burn out the deadly germs, and who knows but that there may be a partial recovery to manhood maimed and scarred and dwarfed, but yet with enough of soil left for the seed of truth that long time may begin the new growth.

Soon, for many of you, youth will pass, and old age come. To those who have borne for many years the heat and burden of the day the signs of the approaching end must be welcome. When the traveler nears the shores of Europe in search of health and recovery he welcomes the indications that he is nearing historic lands and great cities and the capitals of old civilisations. In that moment he forgets the books and games with which he has filled the days of the long and sometimes nauseating voyage. Many of us are approaching another, the unseen continent. Those occupations and professions with which you have filled in your years will soon lose their charm. You have forgotten the trifles of a day and remember the permanent things that shall abide death itself. It is better so. Nothing but good can befall a good man, here or beyond. And other groups have still a long march over the continent of the years. Beware, then, of over-stressing the things that pass. Guard against avarice and consuming ambition. Take time for your friendships. Keep the best wine of life's feast for those to whom you owe the most. Make yourself to mean so much of happiness to those that love you that when you pass it will be as if a star had fallen out of the sky.

Some men there are that bulk little in the body, but they have compacted such treasure of character that the mere entrance into their presence is as if one had come out of the night and the storm into a warm, bright room. Some men are as depressing as a mass of black ice on a northern hillside, and others there are whose very presence makes you think of the shadow of a great rock in life's weary land. Your industry is but the scaffolding of your life. Soon the scaffolding will be pulled down, but the structure of thought and feeling will abide. The real treasure of your life is not that which lies back of you. Your life is in the future. Yesterday is the granary, holding the seed for the morrow's sowing, but the future holds the moist fields. Yesterday holds all the brilliant threads, but today is weaving the glorious texture of character that shall outlast purple and silk of the morrow. Blessed is the man who can serenely look back to yesterday, who works wisely in his today but realises that his real possessions are in the future, across whose threshold we are all today slowly moving.

Printed in the United States of America